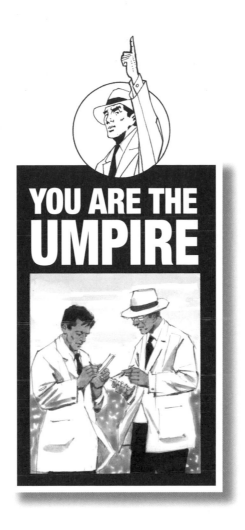

'John Holder is one of the world's best umpires. Plenty of times we've sat down after a game and shared a beer – he loves the sport, and he sets a great example to players and future umpires. He knows it's not a crime to enjoy the game, even if you're one of the guys in charge. All the best umpires know when to have a laugh and a bit of banter, and when not to. That's the spirit behind this book.'

Shane Warne

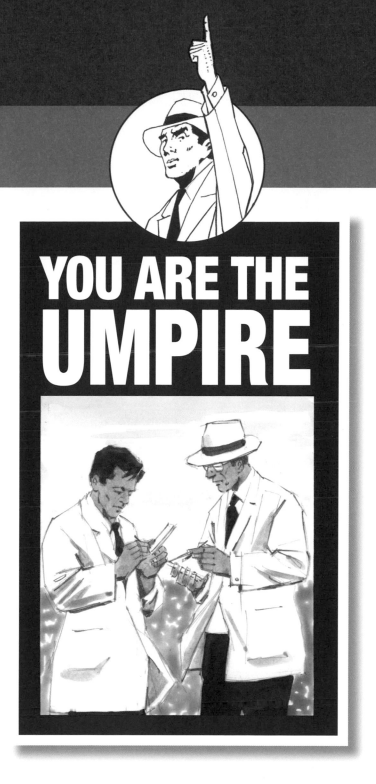

YOU ARE THE UMPIRE

Edited by Giles Richards and David Hills

TheObserver

Published by Observer Books 2009
4 6 8 10 9 7 5

First published in Great Britain in 2009 by
Observer Books
Kings Place
90 York Way
London N1 9GU

www.guardianbooks.co.uk

A CIP catalogue record for this book
is available from the British Library

ISBN 978-0-85265-077-6

Designed and set by www.carrstudio.co.uk
Edited by Giles Richards and David Hills
Contributors: Charlie Nutbrown, Philip Cornwall
Picture editor: Steven Bloor

Printed and bound in Great Britain by Butler Tanner & Dennis Ltd, Frome, Somerset

PICTURE CREDITS

Photographs: Getty Images p6, 9 left, 32, 42, 63 left, 73 left and right, 77 left, 96, 105, 121 top;
Tom Jenkins/Guardian p7, 17, 77 right, 93 right, 106, 107, 119; Philip Brown p11 top;
Associated Press p11 bottom; Paul McFegan/Sportsphoto/Allstar p16; Press Association p23,
47 right, 104, 121 bottom, 123; Patrick Eagar p33, 37 left, 63 right; S&G/Barratts/Press
Association p37 right; Sportphoto p47 left; Hulton-Deutsch/CORBIS p53, 57, 67; Hulton
Archive/Getty Images p82, 118 top; Graham Morris p93 left; Laurence Griffiths/Getty p103;
Rischgitz/Getty Images p116, 117; The Oval p120; Rex Features p 122

CONTENTS

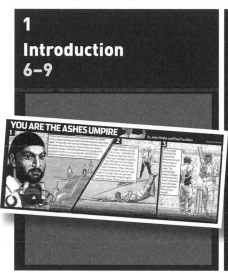

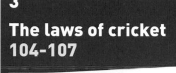
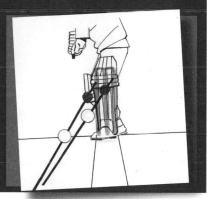

FOREWORD

Shane Warne

I've had my moments with umpires. There's no hiding that. I'd call them disagreements rather than arguments, but it's definitely been lively over the years. But I can also say, hand on heart, I have total respect for the job they do.

In my career I've been lucky to play under some of the best – guys who make the job look simple. People like Peter Willey, David Shepherd, Steve Bucknor, Neil Mallender, Len King and John Holder.

But I've also experienced the negative side – the ones who get it wrong. Umpires who aren't consistent, who can't engage – and some who take the game so seriously it's silly. I'll never forget being asked out the back by a certain umpire, who'll remain nameless. Fortunately, those guys have all retired now. All the current umpires are great…

So what makes a good umpire? For me, the key is an ability to communicate. To avoid behaving like a headmaster. The best umpires are calm, cool, and their decision making is awesome, even in the most intense situations – and even with guys like me on their case. They're full of common sense, concentration and composure, and it's easy to respect them. When they make a mistake, players accept it. A good umpire has everyone working together, not a 'them and us' atmosphere.

John Holder is one of the world's best. He has always been a top decision maker, and he's an excellent guy to talk cricket with. Plenty of times we've sat down after a game and shared a beer – he loves the sport, and he sets a great example to players and future umpires. He knows it's not a crime to enjoy the game, even if you're one of the guys in charge. All the best umpires know when to have a laugh and a bit of banter, and when not to. That's the spirit behind this book.

You Are The Umpire will also fill an important gap. Growing up, I remember picking up the laws of cricket from older players and mates. Only once, when I became captain of my school team, did I read the laws cover to cover. It wasn't much of a laugh. You Are The Umpire can help youngsters learn the game and enjoy it – opening the laws up to different generations.

I also hope it'll increase awareness that umpiring is the hardest job on the pitch – and how that pressure keeps building with every advance in TV replay technology.

People need to recognise that and the status of the top umpires should be elevated: they should be paid the same as players, and given the same respect.

So – would I ever become one? Never say never – but never! It's too intense for me and I'd be rubbish at dealing with players who take it too seriously. But I do have total respect for people like John, and for everyone who takes up this challenge. You can't have good cricket without good umpires.

INTRODUCTION

In a village match a cow suddenly steps through a damaged hedge on to the pitch. The batsman strikes the ball, which bounces off the cow's rump and is caught. Is he out?

You Are The Umpire, drawn by sports artist Paul Trevillion and written by top umpire John Holder, first appeared in *The Observer* newspaper in the UK in May 2006. Featuring a series of awkward umpiring dilemmas, it puts you in the heart of the action, and demands you react quickly and accurately. How well do you know the Laws?

The series was inspired by cult-classic football strip *You Are The Ref* – first drawn by Trevillion in 1957 for *The People* newspaper. Along with his work for *Roy of the Rovers*, Trev's 'The Ref' became famous across the UK, subsequently appearing in *Shoot!* magazine in the 60s and 70s. From 2006, it appeared in *The Observer* and on guardian.co.uk.

After a big public response, Paul decided it was time to diversify. That summer, for the first time in 50 years, *You Are The Ref* took on a new sport, and *You Are The Umpire* was born.

'I'm a huge cricket fan,' says Paul. 'When *The Observer* agreed to run the strip, I called England coach Peter Moores and asked him for some advice on which umpire to approach to work with me. John Holder was the first name off his lips. So I phoned John, and he loved the idea. In the years since we've had a great working relationship. Not only is John as mad keen on cricket as I am, he's also the ultimate professional.'

This book – which follows the 2006 title *You Are The Ref: 50 years of Paul Trevillion's Cult Classic Comic Strip* – is a complete collection of The Ref's younger offshoot. Taking in all of cricket's intricacies and quirks, from the basic laws to the more bizarre, *You Are The Umpire* will test your knowledge to the limits.

And that cow? Find out more on page 39.

THE UMPIRE

John Holder, a former player and one of the world's top umpires, was born in St George, Barbados, in March 1945. A right-arm fast-medium pacer for Hampshire between 1968 and 1972, he joined the first-class umpires panel in 1983. John umpired 11 Test matches and 19 one-day internationals, and in 1987 he came up with the concept of the 'bowl-out' to decide tied matches, replacing the coin toss. In 2008 he was appointed by the ICC as their new Umpire Performance Manager for the Americas and Europe – one of five officials appointed to develop elite standard umpires worldwide.

When I was asked to be part of the new cricket version of *You Are The Ref*, it took me about 30 seconds to say yes. In the years since, we've covered so many aspects of the Laws – from the conventional to the bizarre – and the questions just keep coming.

As a member of the MCC's Laws Working Party, I'm used to dealing with queries from all over the world, but the strip has uncovered all sorts of new questions and challenges. The feedback, from young and old, has been tremendous.

And the strip has been testing the professionals, too. In 2007 at Derby, Mark Alleyne, then Gloucestershire's coach, told me that during a rain delay his team had sat in the dressing room trying to answer the questions in that Sunday's *Observer*. They failed miserably. It just shows how useful a book like this can be: a chance to make sure that everyone who loves the game – fans, players, officials – all know the Laws, and understand why umpires do what they do. I also hope it will inspire more youngsters to get involved in umpiring.

It's been wonderful trawling through my memories to help put the book together. I've been lucky to have worked with some of the true greats, and there are so many who stand out. Brian Lara, who took batting to fantastic new heights; Wasim Akram, who was a nightmare to umpire, because his back leg hid his front foot, making it difficult to judge no balls – and of course Shane Warne. In 1993 I umpired Shane for the first time at Canterbury, for Kent v Australia. He spun the ball so hard that you could actually hear it fizz as it left his fingers. He was always lively company too – no one's appeals are more aggressive! It's fantastic to see so many legends like these guys brought to life in Paul Trevillion's amazing artwork.

So what do I hope this book will achieve? Whether you're a budding umpire of the future of just a lover of cricket, I hope it will give you a chance to experience the huge job umpires do. As you ponder some of the questions, remember that real umpires have split seconds to get them right, under huge pressure and often watched by enormous audiences worldwide.

It's a tough, intense, challenging job – but for me, it's also one of the best in the world.

THE ARTIST

Born in 1934 in Love Lane, in London's Tottenham, Paul Trevillion was always going to be an artist. He was drawing for comics like *Eagle* and *TV21* when he was still at school, and as an adult his work has appeared in almost every UK newspaper, and in magazines from *NME* to the *Radio Times*. Famous for series like *Roy of The Rovers*, he's also the author and illustrator of more than 20 books, and illustrated the *Gary Player Golf Class*, which appeared in over 1,000 newspapers worldwide.

Paul, who spent a large part of his career in the US, is acclaimed as the finest proponent of comic art realism – an expert in accuracy and movement. Disney animator Milt Neil said it took '20 Disney drawings to produce the movement Trevillion captures in one'.

During his career Paul has met and drawn an extraordinary list of sporting greats: Pele, Jack Nicklaus, Sugar Ray Robinson – and many of the modern generation, from Wayne Rooney to Tiger Woods.

Away from art, Trevillion has had a full, proudly different life. Among the highlights: a stand-up career alongside the likes of Tommy Cooper and Norman Wisdom; a record deal; he's been crowned world speed-kissing champion (25,009 in two hours); had coffee with, then drew, Winston Churchill; devised a spilt-handed putting technique; caused uproar by drawing Evonne Goolagong nude for *The Sun*; invented sock tags, made famous by Don Revie's Leeds United team; and dressed up as DJ Bear, the Panda of Peace, in the 1980s – to pacify football hooligans and spread love in the game.

You Are The Ref continues to go from strength to strength in *The Observer* and online, and *You Are The Umpire*, first published in *The Observer* in 2006, has a big following too.

'I'm delighted the "You Are The..." format has survived the test of time, and it's been great to have had the chance to bring it to cricket. I'm a huge cricket fan – as a youngster I supported Middlesex and my position was wicketkeeper: I used to dive around like Godfrey Evans, the greatest keeper I've ever had the privilege of watching.

'But this isn't the first time I've drawn cricket. In 1952 I met the Duke of Edinburgh, who asked about my ambitions. I told him I wanted to draw sports stars for the national press – and he told me: "Then start with the Australian and England cricketers in next year's Test series" – a royal command! Soon after, the *Sporting Record* asked me to do just that, and the rest is history.

'I'm really proud of this book – it's been a privilege to work on. All my artwork here is dedicated to my two team-mates who made it all happen - *The Observer's* Giles Richards and David Hills. No words can match the drama, electricity, anxiety and creativity between the three of us – backed by John Holder's command of the laws – that hammered this book over the boundary line. It was great to play under such inspiring leadership.'

Shane Warne

Full name: Shane Keith Warne
Date of birth: September 13, 1969
Teams: Australia, Victoria, Hampshire

Tests: 145	ODIs: 194
Ave: 17.32	Ave: 13.05
Fifties: 12	Fifties: 1
Wickets: 708	Wickets: 293
Bowling ave: 25.41	Bowling ave: 25.73
BBI*: 8-71	BBM: 5-33
BBM†: 12-128	

Player statistics correct to November 2008
*Best Bowling In Innings †Best Bowling In Match

Controversial and charismatic, Warne was arguably the greatest international bowler of all-time. Although Muttiah Muralitharan (see page 78) has since passed his 708 Test wickets to set a new Test record, Warne's place in the history books is secure. Single-handedly reinventing leg-spin, he turned the delivery from a defensive art into the most glamorous of all cricketing roles. His armoury was replete with sliders, zooters, googlies – all sorts of deliveries that created a formidable aura around him. And that image was part of his success: he made the legend that surrounded him into one of his greatest assets, often dismissing batsmen with deliveries they would have played comfortably had they come from anyone else's hand.

His career was not without incident, to put it mildly. In 1991 his dedication to hedonism resulted in his expulsion from the Australian academy and, later, sex, drug and bookmaking scandals tarnished his personal reputation. While these incidents added to his cult-hero image, they prevented him from becoming Australia captain, a role that he craved and, it's generally agreed, at which he would have excelled. Nevertheless, his genius was undiminished, and his position in the pantheon of greats was confirmed when he was voted one of the five Wisden Cricketers of the Twentieth Century.

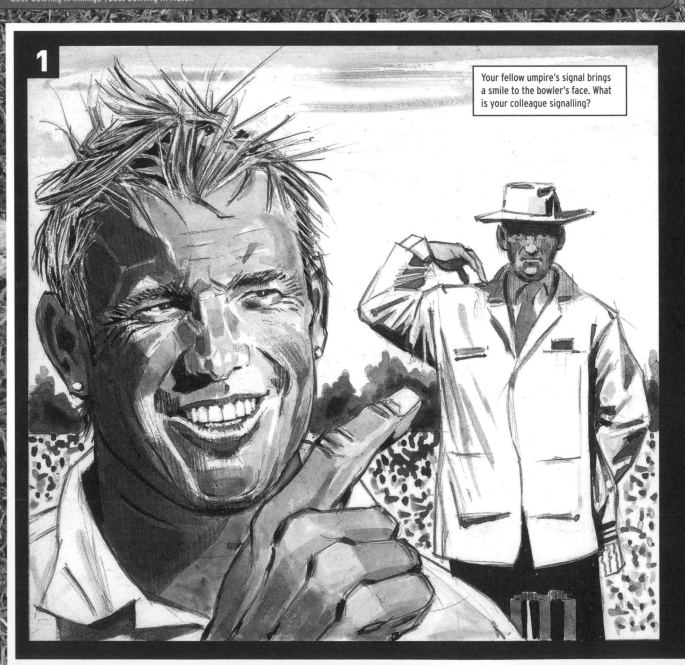

1

Your fellow umpire's signal brings a smile to the bowler's face. What is your colleague signalling?

2

At Canterbury (in the old days, before the big tree died) a ball strikes the upper branches of the tree but still clears the boundary. What do you give?

TREVILLION—

3

A batsman's bat breaks in half mid-shot. He trips on the piece of broken blade, knocking it back into the stumps. Is he out hit wicket?

Answers

1) He's signalling 'one short'. If a batsman fails to step inside or ground the bat inside the popping crease at the end of a run, the umpire signals 'one short' and the run does not count.

2) Four runs. The tree inside the boundary at Canterbury counted as part of the boundary. Therefore if the ball struck any part of it, even though it landed over the boundary, it's not a six and a four must be awarded.

3) Yes, he's out hit wicket. If, in playing a shot or setting off for a run, any part of a batsman's person or equipment breaks the wicket then he's out on appeal. But it would have been better – if there was time – to signal 'dead ball' once you realised neither batsman was looking for a run. That might have stopped the striker tripping on the bat and breaking his wicket.

A batsman is struck on the helmet. Dazed, he walks into his stumps. The fielding team appeal. What do you decide?

1

A batsman is struck on the helmet. Dazed, he walks into his stumps. The fielding team appeal. What do you decide?

TREVILLION

Answers

1) As soon as you realise the batsman is hurt call 'dead ball' to stop any further development. If, though, the batsman breaks his wicket, then, on appeal, he is out hit wicket. You can ask the fielding captain if he wants the appeal to stand – if he does, it must be upheld.

2) Other than at the end of an innings, a bowler must complete an over in progress unless he's injured or suspended under any of the laws. But you're not a doctor: if a captain says his bowler is injured, you must allow another player to take over.

3) On appeal, the injured batsman is out. An injured striker with a runner must, at all times, remain in his ground, behind the popping crease. The moment he leaves his ground, and the wicket is broken at the wicketkeeper's end, he's run out regardless of where his runner is.

2

In a village match, a bowler sends down a series of wides and no balls, making for an impossibly long over. He's fit to continue bowling, but his captain wants to take him off with a couple of balls left in the over. What do you do?

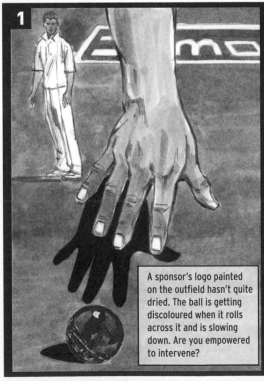

A sponsor's logo painted on the outfield hasn't quite dried. The ball is getting discoloured when it rolls across it and is slowing down. Are you empowered to intervene?

1

2

The wicketkeeper moves to collect a throw-in with both batsmen stranded at the other end of the wicket – but just before he collects the ball he accidentally dislodges a bail. The wicketkeeper collects the ball then breaks the wicket and appeals – but the batsman insists he's not run out because the ball became 'dead' when the keeper dislodged a bail. What is your decision?

Andrew Flintoff

Full name: Andrew 'Freddie' Flintoff
Date of birth: December 6, 1977
Teams: England, Lancashire

Tests: 70	ODIs: 138
Ave: 32.35	Ave: 32.6
Fifties: 24	Fifties: 18
Centuries: 5	Centuries: 3
High score: 167	High score: 123
Wickets: 206	Wickets: 163
Bowling ave: 32.21	Bowling ave: 24.69
BBI: 5-58 BBM: 8-156	BBM: 5-56

After Ian Botham's retirement, English cricket produced a parade of 'new Bothams'. None, however, was worthy of the tag until 'Freddie' came to prominence. An all-rounder of immense talent, Flintoff's initial international career was underwhelming: overweight and under-motivated, his partying was more prolific than his run scoring. But a scolding by the Lancashire management and a spell at Rod Marsh's ECB academy provided the jolt he needed.

Freddie soon proved himself to be a world-class all-rounder. Tall and muscular, he's a destructive, though erratic, middle-order batsman who has bludgeoned more sixes in Tests and ODIs than any other Englishman. As a bowler, his ability to bowl tightly while coercing reverse swing at over 90mph ensures that he can operate as both a stock and strike bowler. His role in the victorious 2005 Ashes cemented his position at the top of international cricket and, despite suffering from injuries, Flintoff has established himself as one of England's great all-rounders.

3 In a tense finish to a one-day international, an injured batsman who has been making use of a runner gets overexcited and sets off for a quick single – outpacing his runner. The batsman gets home in time, but the runner is short of his ground when the stumps are broken at the wicketkeeper's end. What do you decide?

3 A fielder racing to stop a ball reaching the boundary bends over sharply to try to pick it up. As he does so his hat falls off and the ball rolls over it, slowing it down enough to stop it crossing the boundary. What do you decide?

TREVILLION

Answers

1) Yes, you have the authority to have the logo covered. Anything that will damage the ball or potentially be dangerous for players can be put right by umpires.

2) He's out. As long as one ball remains on top of the stumps, removing that is enough for the run out to count.

3) This is not illegal fielding – it was accidental. But if he had thrown his hat and the ball struck it while it was live, that would constitute illegal fielding and five penalty runs would be awarded.

Sajid Mahmood

Full name: Sajid Iqbal Mahmood
Date of birth: December 21, 1981
Teams: England, Lancashire

Tests: 8	ODIs: 25
Ave: 8.10	Ave: 7.72
Wickets: 20	Wickets: 29
Bowling ave: 38.10	Bowling ave: 38.89
BBI: 4-22 BBM: 6-130	BBM: 4-50

Sajid Mahmood's rise was as rapid and unpredictable as his bowling. In 2003 he was selected for the England 'A' side despite having only six first class wickets to his name, and the following year he made his ODI debut. However he was perhaps selected too soon, as his seven overs against New Zealand went for 56 runs with no return. But in 2006 he made his full Test debut, and did so with more success: his first four overs collected three wickets.

Mahmood's early England career was aided by the England hierarchy's belief that genuine speed was necessary for an international fast bowler. Speed has never been Mahmood's worry: bowling at around 90mph, he can swing the ball wildly and, with his height and his habit of pitching fuller than standard, he's occasionally unplayable. Unfortunately, his lack of control and a typically mixed 2007 World Cup resulted in him being dropped.

Kevin Pietersen

Full name: Kevin Peter Pietersen
Date of birth: June 27, 1980
Teams: England, KwaZulu-Natal,
Nottinghamshire, Hampshire

Tests: 43	ODIs: 87
Ave: 50.51	Ave: 48.36
Fifties: 11	Fifties: 20
Centuries: 14	Centuries: 7
High score: 226	High score: 116

Having grown disgruntled with his home nation's quota system, South-Africa born Kevin Pietersen, whose mother is English, chose to play for England instead. It was a controversial decision, but the Proteas' loss was definitely the Three Lions' gain. An unorthodox, swashbuckling batsman, Pietersen is one of the most dangerous cricketers in the game. Although capable of playing classically and of defending with a flourish, KP is generally associated with wristy flicks through leg, charges down the pitch, and ferociously clean hitting. In 2008 he unveiled a new shot, the switch-hit, in which he reverses his stance at the moment of delivery to effectively bat left-handed.

Pietersen made his ODI debut, fittingly, on a tour of South African. Booed by the crowd and castigated by the home media, he revelled in the situation and scored three centuries. Since then he has become a Test player of true stature, scoring more runs in his first 25 Tests than all but Donald Bradman. But his obvious self-confidence has a downside too. In August 2008 he was appointed both the Test and one-day captain – but in January 2009 resigned after a series of clashes with coach Peter Moores.

1

A batsman hits a ball that will clear the boundary for a six. But it strikes a bird in flight: the ball drops down just inside the boundary and is caught. What do you decide?

Answers

1) The fact that the ball struck the bird is unlucky for the batsman (and for the bird...) and could be called an act of God. Because the ball has not touched the ground the decision is out on appeal.

2) No. By law, the maximum width of the bat is 4.25 inches, so anything wider isn't allowed.

3) You, as an umpire, are part of play, so despite the deflection, you'd give the batsman run out on appeal. Equally, if the ball is driven by the striker, hits either umpire and is caught by a fielder before hitting the ground, he is out on appeal.

1

In a competitive U14 game, the striker hits the ball high into the air. The non-striker sees a fielder is about to catch it so shouts 'Drop it!' just as he goes to take the catch. He does indeed fail to make the catch and the fielding side appeal angrily. What is your decision?

TREVILLION-

Answers

1) You would give the striking batsman out, caught; the offending non-striker would be reported for obstruction and five penalty runs would be awarded to the fielding side. Obstruction can be physical – where a fielder deliberately gets in the way of either batsman or vice versa. But it can also be the act of verbally distracting an opponent. The ball will not count in the over and the offending player will be reported to the authorities.

2

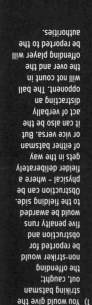

It is the last ball of a limited overs match and the scores are level. The batting side have one wicket left. The last ball is delivered down the leg side and you call the ball a wide. However the batsman has moved out of his crease towards the ball and is stumped. What is your decision?

2 A powerfully built batsman, over 6ft tall, walks to the crease with a purpose-made bat with a blade that is six inches wide. The wicketkeeper protests that the bat is illegal. Do you let him use it?

3 A batsman hammers the ball along the ground and the bowler attempts to stop it with his boot. The ball ricochets off his foot, strikes your boot and is deflected into the wicket, removing both bails. The non-striker, who was backing up, is out of the crease. Do you give him out?

TREVILLION.

Wilfred Rhodes

Full name: Wilfred Rhodes
Date of birth: October 29, 1877
Major teams: England, Yorkshire

Tests: 58	Wickets: 127
Ave: 30.19	Bowling
Centuries: 2	ave: 26.96
Fifties: 11	BBI: 8-68
High score: 179	BBM: 15-124

Wilfred Rhodes' figures prove what an extraordinary cricketer he was. His total of 4,204 first-class wickets remains a record, he played in more first-class matches (1,110) and more County Championship matches (763) than any other player, he took 100 wickets in a season a record 23 times, and achieved the double (1,000 runs and 100 wickets) on a record 16 occasions. The stats are evidence both of his talent and his admirable persistence: his Test career spanned 31 years.

He started his career with Yorkshire as a left arm orthodox bowler – never a massive turner of the ball, he bowled low, flat and accurately. But through hard work he turned himself into one of the great all-rounders: having begun his Test career batting at 11, he eventually formed a fine opening partnership for England with Jack Hobbs. He pioneered the full-frontal stance and his batting – not the most elegant – could prove hugely effective. His tally of two Test centuries doesn't really do justice to his quality: but his 30,000 runs for Yorkshire certainly does. He died in 1973.

3 A batsman goes for a quick single but the fielder throws the ball at the wicket and flattens the stumps. However the batsman was just safe and you disallow the appeal for run-out. The ball, meanwhile, has shot off into the deep and the batsmen run again. Does the extra run count?

Answers

2) It is a victory for the batting side. They will have won by one wicket the moment you call wide. At that point the one run they needed to win has been scored and the match has ended, making the stumping irrelevant.

3) Yes the run is valid because the ball is still live, even after it had broken the wicket. It would have become dead, however, if you had given the run-out.

1

The ball beats the batsman and hits the off stump, making one bail jump two inches into the air. But it lands back in position on the stumps. The bowler, convinced he has broken the wicket, appeals. The batsman insists he's not out as the wicket is intact. What is your decision?

Monty Panesar

Full name: Mudhsuden Singh Panesar
Date of birth: April 25, 1982
Teams: England, Northamptonshire

Tests: 33	ODIs: 26
Ave: 5.50	Ave: 5.20
Wickets: 114	Wickets: 24
Bowling ave: 31.95	Bowling ave: 40.83
BBI: 6-37	BBM: 3-25
BBM: 10-187	

The first Sikh to play for England, Monty Panesar is a slow left-arm orthodox spinner who uses his height and large hands to create massive degrees of spin. Attacking yet accurate, Panesar has the ability to both block an end, as shown by an economy rate of 2.83, and to be his team's spearhead.

Panesar was first selected for the tour to India in March 2006, and marked his arrival with the wicket of Sachin Tendulkar, his childhood hero. While a permanent spot in the England team was initially barred by then-coach Duncan Fletcher's preference for multi-dimensional cricketers, Panesar soon established himself as an England mainstay. His distinctive appearance, trademark celebrations and comically inept fielding and batting have helped him become a cult crowd favourite. A simple stop in the field or a single run from his bat usually whips up a mighty cheer. However, the humour is both affectionate and respectful: Monty Panesar has proven himself England's most talented spinner for a generation.

2

A batsman, attempting a sweep shot, gets a top edge and, seeing the ball is going to fall on his stumps, knocks it away with his bat. The fielding side appeal for 'hit ball twice'. What's your decision?

3

A first-class county side, with a long journey to undertake to play the next day, rattle up a quick 300 against Scotland in a one-day tournament. Their captain declares, hoping for an early finish so they can get on the road. What do you do?

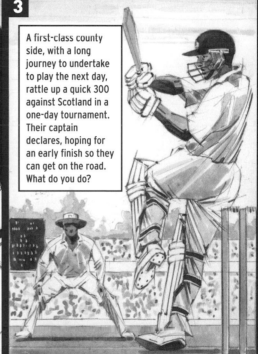

Answers

1) Not out. There have been many instances of the ball striking the stumps and one ball, or even both, jumping into the air and then settling back into the groove on top of the stumps, but the bail or bails must be permanently removed for it to count as a dismissal.

2) Not out. A batsman defending his wicket can legally knock the ball away with his bat or any part of his body, except the hand that is not holding the bat. However if, in knocking the ball away, he prevents a catch from being taken, he will be given out, on appeal, for obstruction.

3) They must bat on. In one-day cricket there is a regulation outlawing declaration at county level.

1

You signal a wide, but the wicketkeeper, still able to collect the ball, stumps the batsman while he's out of his crease and appeals. The batsman doesn't move, insisting you can't be stumped off a wide. What is your decision?

2

In the last session under a darkening sky, you offer the batsmen the light. The batsmen, chasing a small target, want to play on but the fielding captain insists that, in the gloom, it's hard to pick up the ball when it comes off the bat and that it's too dangerous to continue. What is your decision?

Muttiah Muralitharan

Full name: Muttiah Muralitharan
Date of birth: April 17, 1972
Teams: Sri Lanka, Kandurata, Kent, Lancashire.

Tests: 123	ODIs: 318
Ave: 11.33	Ave: 5.94
Fifties: 1	Wickets: 490
Wickets: 756	Bowling ave: 22.64
Bowling ave: 21.96	BBM: 7-30
BBI: 9-51 BBM: 16-220	

Despite having taken more wickets at a cheaper rate in both Tests and ODIs, Muralitharan's career has been unfairly overshadowed by Shane Warne's. It was only deep into their respective careers that there was widespread recognition that the Sri Lankan was just as touched by genius as the Australian. The under-appreciation stemmed from two misconceptions: that Murali takes his wickets against weaker nations, and that his action is illegal.

While it's true that Murali took 163 wickets at a ridiculous 14.57 against Bangladesh and Zimbabwe, his average is lower than Warne's against every team except Pakistan. Controversies over his action, however, have undeniably blighted his career. He was called for throwing in Australia in 1995, although ICC tests later cleared his action. The debate comes because of an involuntarily bent arm and a double-jointed wrist – a combination that results in a vicious off-break, a top-spinner that slides straight, and a doosra that breaks away from his stock ball. But with a world record number of international wickets already, including a record 756 in Tests, the history books have settled the argument.

1

You're umpiring a Test Match at the same time as a World Cup football game goes to penalties. The crowd, listening to the football on radios, are more interested in the penalties than the cricket and their noisy reactions are distracting the players. Can you suspend play?

3

Off the last ball of an over, the bowler strikes the batsman full on the pad. On the changeover, the wicketkeeper tells the bowler that the batsman was plump lbw. The bowler believes that because the umpire has called 'over' it's too late to appeal, but the keeper insists he's wrong. Who is right?

TREVILLION

Answers

1) Give the batsman out: Law 25 states that you can be stumped off a wide.

2) Umpires have a duty of care to both teams and themselves, so in this case you would suspend play. If conditions are so bad as to pose a serious risk of injury to the participants, then play can be stopped and not restarted until that risk disappears.

3) The wicketkeeper is in the right: give the batsman out on appeal. Any member of the fielding side can appeal after the call of 'over', but it must be done before the next bowler starts his run-up.

Paul Collingwood

Full name: Paul David Collingwood
Date of birth: May 26, 1976
Teams: England, Durham

Tests: 39	ODIs: 154
Ave: 42.01	Ave: 34.30
Centuries: 6	Centuries: 4
Fifties: 11	Fifties: 20
High score: 206	Wickets: 84
Wickets: 17	Bowling ave: 38.95
Bowling ave: 49.07	

Never marked for greatness, Collingwood has always had to fight for respect and his international place, a feat he first achieved in the ODI arena – where his medium pace is useful enough to qualify him as an all-rounder – and then, after several false starts, in the Test team. His Test place was only truly consolidated during the 2006-07 Ashes when he hit 206 at Adelaide, becoming only the third Englishman to make a double century in Australia.

Though his batting in Tests is usually more stolid than exceptional, his exploits in the one day game have shown that he can be a devastating shot-maker. The transformation in his public image was completed when, in 2007, he was roundly considered the only viable option for one-day captain. However, he found the pressures of the position hampered his form and he resigned and returned to the ranks in 2008. One area of his game over which there have never been doubts is his fielding. Whether at backward point, cover or slip, Collingwood's agility and speed have made him a latter-day Jonty Rhodes.

2

A fielder throws, trying for a quick run-out, but his aim is way off-line: the ball hits the running batsman's shoulder and is deflected on to the wicket, removing both bails. What is your decision?

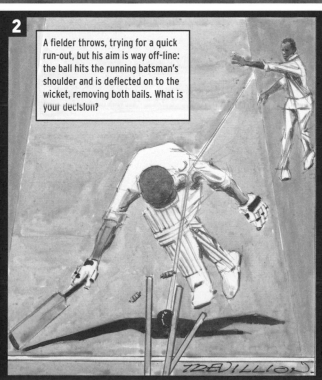

TREVILLION

3

An injured fielder is replaced by a twelfth man who excels at cover point. When he adopts this position in the field, both batsmen object and insist he fields further away from the bat, preferably at third man. What is your decision?

Answers

1) Yes, you can suspend play. Ask the ground authority to make an announcement over the public-address system outlining what the problem is and asking for a reduction in noise.

2) Run out on appeal, if he hasn't reached his ground. The batsman is part of play: the same would apply if it deflected off either umpire – you're also part of play.

3) The batting side's captain has no power to object to where a substitute fields. Obviously, the fielding captain will put him wherever he wants, hit under the Laws of Cricket 2000 code he cannot keep wicket. This doesn't refer to county cricket, because a special regulation allows a sub to keep wicket.

David Gower

Full name: David Ivon Gower
Date of birth: April 1, 1957
Teams: England, Leicestershire, Hampshire

Tests: 117	ODIs: 114
Ave: 44.25	Ave: 30.77
Centuries: 18	Centuries: 7
Fifties: 39	Fifties: 12
High score: 215	High score: 158

An elegant left-handed batsman, Gower thrilled and frustrated in equal measure. Much was expected of the sort of rare talent who could pull his first ball in Test cricket to the square-leg boundary. However the accusation that followed him was that he was a player who liked to score stylish vignettes – and took what seemed to be a casual, lackadaisical approach.

But that's unfair. A player who scored 18 Test centuries, who is third in his country's appearance table and who once broke the record for the most Test runs by an Englishman – and did it, typically, with an ethereal cover drive – can't be said to have wasted his talent. His reputation for indifference on the field was probably the product of his manner off it: his laid-back character wasn't a great fit in an age of increased professionalism. But he captained England in 32 Tests, leading his team to victory in the 1985 Ashes, and today he is hugely respected in the sport. The same qualities that made him a frustrating player to watch have since made him an urbane and engaging broadcaster.

1 In an attempt to change his luck, a captain who has suffered an exceptionally long run at losing the toss asks if he can step back into cricket history and, instead of tossing a coin, throw a bat into the air and call which way the face will land – sky or grass. What's your decision?

Ricky Ponting

Full name: Ricky Thomas Ponting
Date of birth: December 19, 1974
Teams: Australia, Tasmania

Tests: 125	ODIs: 301
Ave: 57.18	Ave: 43.24
Centuries: 36	Centuries: 26
Fifties: 42	Fifties: 64
High score: 257	High score: 164

With 36 Test centuries and an average pushing 60, Ricky Ponting is on his way to becoming an all-time great. Of his fellow countrymen only Donald Bradman and Michael Hussey average higher, and, of all Test players, only Sachin Tendulkar has passed 100 more often. A top-order batsmen with both style and brutality, Ponting's aggressive stroke-play is equally well suited to the shortened form of the game: he has scored the fifth most ODI runs and the third most ODI centuries ever.

Ponting made his debut at the age of 20 and, aside from a publicly acknowledged alcohol problem, his rise from precocious teenager to Australia captain has been faultless. The only stumble was the 2005 Ashes loss – Australia's first for 18 years. However, he recovered

1 A fielder positions himself so that his shadow falls across the pitch, where a slow bowler is pitching the ball. As the bowler runs in the fielder doesn't stay still – the shadow of his upper body moves from side to side. The batsman insists he's a distraction and asks you to remove him. What is your decision?

Answers

1) If you decide that the fielder is moving deliberately to distract the batsman, you should call 'dead ball', warn the fielding captain that it is illegal and that they're liable to five penalty runs. The fielder's shadow being on the pitch in itself is not a problem, but if he is moving once the ball is delivered you have to take action. Instruct the captain to move the offender away.

2) Not out. You have to be absolutely certain that the catcher had control of the ball and was able to dispose of it. There's no time limit for the catcher to hold the ball: your decision must be based solely on whether he had control.

3) In this case award six runs if you think, before the interception occurred, the ball would have cleared the boundary. Before the start of play, umpires and captains together decide on what the boundaries are. If they decide an interception like this constitutes a boundary then they must judge whether to award a four or a six.

his form and his authority, and since that defeat he has averaged over 70 in Tests. He has grown as a captain, too, and has now presided over back-to-back World Cup wins, and the

2

A batsman with a purpose-made, very low-cut glove is struck on the wrist. A fielder catches the ball and appeals. The batsman points to the red mark on his wrist and stands his ground. Do you give the batsman out?

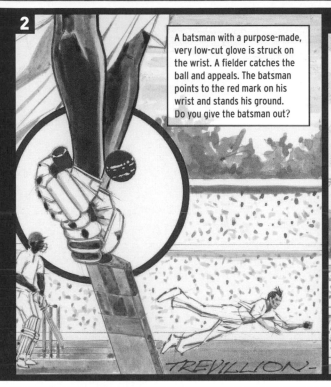

3

A batsman runs halfway down the pitch in an attempt to hammer a slow bowler over the sight screen, but in his eagerness he mistimes the ball and it strikes him in the middle of the helmet. The bowler appeals for lbw. What is your decision?

TREVILLION-

Answers

1) If the other captain agrees, allow him to use this old-fashioned method. There was a time when, in charity matches, the Lord Mayor would be asked to do the toss and would use a special coin – that's probably how the practice of using a coin rather than the bat arose.

2) No. Unless you're certain that the ball has struck the hand (not the wrist) you cannot award the wicket.

3) Not out. The further the batsman is from the stumps the more uncertainty there is regarding lbw. In this case he's too far advanced for you to be sure that the ball would have hit the wicket.

2

A batsman who has passed 200 unexpectedly offers up a dolly catch. An overjoyed fielder collects the ball and in the same movement throws it up in the air, but drops it when it comes down. The batsman stands his ground, insisting the fielder did not close his fingers over the ball – that it was a knock into the air that he dropped. What is your decision?

TREVILLION.

3

A batsman hitting six after six has the delighted crowd catching the ball as it clears the boundary ropes. In all the excitement a fan runs forward to catch the ball and steps over the boundary. He fails to catch the ball, only succeeding in knocking it into the crowd. What do you give?

first Ashes whitewash for 86 years. With the retirement of Brian Lara and the decline of Sachin Tendulkar, he is the pre-eminent batsman in world cricket.

WG Grace

Full name: William Gilbert Grace
Date of birth: July 18, 1848
Teams: England, Gloucestershire

Tests: 22
Ave: 32.29
Centuries: 2
Fifties: 5

High score: 170
Wickets: 9
Bowling ave: 26.22
BBM: 3-68

1

The fielding captain, desperately in need of a wicket, instructs his keeper to hand over his gloves and pads to first slip to keep wicket so he can come on to bowl – explaining to you that, in 1896, WG Grace brought on his wicketkeeper, AA Lilley, to bowl: Lilley took a wicket then went back behind the stumps. Do you allow it?

WG Grace's Test stats fail to give an accurate picture of his talent and influence.

Though primarily remembered as the first modern batsman, he was a truly great all-rounder. He scored an astonishing 54,211 first-class runs with 124 centuries and 251 fifties, took 2,809 wickets at an average of 18.14, and was a supremely athletic fielder at point or cover. He also remains the first person to take a catch with the first ball faced as a wicketkeeper in Test cricket. His innovation as a batsman, inventing many of the modern batting techniques, stands in contrast to his persistence with round-arm bowling. It's unfortunate that Grace didn't make his Test debut until the age of 32, when he was no longer at his imperious best.

Known solely by his initials and instantly recognised by his iconic beard, Grace was one of the pre-eminent figures of his day and his fame spread beyond cricket. Despite doing so much for the sport, he was definitely 'not cricket': legends abound of gamesmanship, even cheating, and his irascible and mercenary temperament. Nevertheless, in terms of influence and fame, he has few peers in the history of cricket. He died in 1915.

2

A bowler with an exceptionally long follow through is annoyed as the batsman snicks the ball and sets off for a quick single. He remains in the direct path of the batsman, making no effort to move, and they collide, resulting in a run-out. The batsman insists he was obstructed. What is your decision?

3

A fielder, attempting a high catch, fails to hold the ball, falls awkwardly and doesn't get up. He's obviously hurt, but the ball is still in play. Do you wait for another fielder to run over and return the ball to the wicketkeeper and then assess the injury or deny the batsmen any further runs and stop play immediately?

TREVILLION-

Answers

1) Allow the change – there's no law against changing the wicketkeeper. However, you must watch out for time-wasting – in a close game with time running out this could be a ploy to prevent the batting side from winning.

2) You must decide whether the obstruction was deliberate. A bowler is allowed to follow through along his normal course and it is the batsman's duty to run around him. If you think it wasn't intentional then the batsman is out. If it was deliberate you should call 'dead ball' immediately and award five penalty runs to the batting side. The ball will not count in the over and the incident will be reported. Something similar happened in the early Nineties in a B&H match between Hampshire and Nottinghamshire. Paul Terry drove a ball from Kevin Evans to mid-on and set off for a quick single. As he ran he watched the ball and collided with the bowler who, in his follow through, had turned sharply to watch the ball. They collided and run-out was correctly given on appeal.

3) Stop play immediately. As soon as either umpire realises that the player is hurt he will call 'dead ball'. The runs completed before the incident or the umpire's call, plus the run in progress if the batsmen have crossed, will count.

Mike Brearley

Full name: John Michael Brearley
Date of birth: April 28, 1942
Major teams: England,
Middlesex

Tests: 39		ODIs: 25	
Ave: 22.88		Ave: 24.28	
Centuries: 0		Centuries: 0	
Fifties: 9		Fifties: 3	
High score: 91		High score: 78	

Rarely can a sportsman be so hailed and so derided simultaneously. A batsman who never scored a Test century in 39 Tests, Brearley wouldn't have merited his position in the England team if it wasn't for one exceptional talent: his captaincy. He became a specialist captain, with his powers of leadership, his understanding of psychology and his tactical acumen deemed to outweigh his shortage of runs. He was once famously described as having a 'degree in people'.

He was first appointed captain in 1977, but it was the 1981 Ashes series that cemented his reputation. He succeeded Ian Botham and managed to revive a moribund England team, galvanising them – and Beefy particularly – to such an extent that that they overturned a deficit and performed several seemingly impossible comebacks to clinch one of the most remarkable series ever. In 1985 he published *The Art of Captaincy*, which remains the definitive work on cricket tactics. He now works as a psychoanalyst, a psychotherapist, a cricket writer for *The Observer* newspaper, and as the President of the MCC.

1 A batsman whacks a loose ball long and high: you watch in amazement as it lands plumb on the boundary rope and bounces back up into the chasing fielder's hands. Is it a) 4; b) 6; or c) out, caught?

1 A player gives you his mobile phone to look after. You think it's off, but it rings as the bowler is in his delivery stride. The batsman misses the ball and is bowled middle stump – but claims he was put off by the ring. What do you do?

2 A fast bowler has his shirt unbuttoned a long way down. The batsman claims his shirt collar is flapping as he bowls and is distracting him – he demands the bowler buttons it up. What is your decision?

2

A batsman gives a faint edge to the ball, which is caught by the wicketkeeper. He walks immediately out of his crease towards the pavilion, but then realises nobody has appealed, so turns round and walks back to resume his innings. Do you allow it?

3

The scoreboard shows that a team have scored 400 runs in a County Championship match. The captain declares as they've earned all their bonus points. But after the terms leave the field, an embarrassed scorer comes up to you and says he has spotted an error and only 399 runs were scored. What do you do?

Answers

1) b) Six runs. Any ball that lands from the bat on, or over, the boundary rope or fence is counted as a six. Though with the boundary rope usually at least 50 yards away, you'd have to be sure that the ball landed exactly on top of it.

3) Yes, allow him to return: a batsman can only be given out on appeal. In this case, although the fielding side believed he was caught and he began to walk, their failure to appeal means he's perfectly entitled to return to the crease.

3) Once a side has declared the decision cannot be revoked. So unfortunately in a case like this, if the scorers were correct and only 399 had been scored, that total would stand and the batting side would not receive the extra bonus points. Because county clubs employ two professional scorers, one for each team, they should be constantly cross-checking for accuracy, making a mistake like this one highly unlikely.

Marcus Trescothick

Full name: Marcus Edward Trescothick
Date of birth: December 25, 1975
Teams: England, Somerset

	Tests: 76	ODIs: 123
	Ave: 43.79	Ave: 37.37
	Centuries: 14	Centuries: 12
	Fifties: 29	Fifties: 21
	High score: 219	High score: 137

With twelve one day centuries to his name, Trescothick is the most successful ODI batsman that England has ever produced. An attacking left-handed opener, famed for his cover drives and pulls, he was, for six years, an equally important component of England's Test side. Apart from a fine 219 against South Africa, the highlight of his Test career was the victorious 2005 Ashes series. Although Banger, as he's known, missed his last chance to notch a century against the Aussies, he did average 43.10 in the series and is credited with providing much of England's confidence and impetus.

Trescothick's England career was curtailed by what he called at the time a 'stress-related illness', which forced him to leave the 2006 tour to India. After an aborted attempt to return for the 2006-07 Ashes, he conceded that he would never play for his country again. He returned to the more relaxed pastures of county cricket and rediscovered his form and enjoyment for Somerset. In 2008 he published an award winning autobiography, *Coming Back to Me*, in which he discussed openly his long-term struggle with anxiety and depression.

3

A player well known for his love of racing offers you a tip for a race during the lunchtime interval. Would it be ethical to back the horse? Would your answer be different if this was after a match was over?

Answers

1) Immediately call and signal dead ball – the wicket does not stand. But this is extremely embarrassing; you shouldn't have let it get this far. If a player asks you to hold his mobile, refuse. The player should make sure it's switched off and either keep it himself or send it off the field.

2) Tell the bowler to button up his shirt. John Holder: This actually happened to me as a player in a friendly match between Hampshire and Sussex in the late 1960s. The Nawab of Pataudi, batting for Sussex, claimed that my shirt, open at the neck, was distracting hiiii as I bowled – the umpire told me to button up.

3) There's no problem betting on horses – but players and officials are advised against betting on the outcome of cricket matches.

1 A batsman plays a smart defensive shot, which drops down and stops dead at his feet. He kindly picks it up and throws it back to the bowler – only to hear the wicketkeeper behind him appeal. What is your decision?

2 The helmet of a close fielder is discarded behind the wicketkeeper. The batsman edges a delivery high above the keeper, who stands on and jumps off the helmet and claims the catch. What do you give?

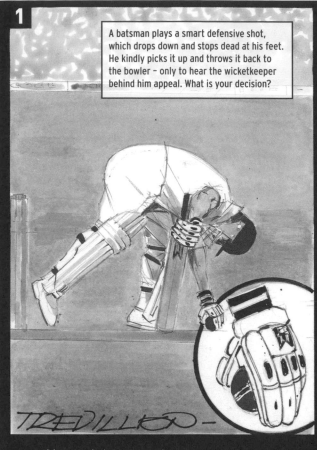

TREDILLION –

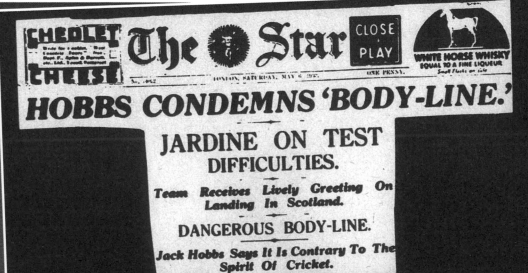

Answers

1) Out – obstruction. Once the striker has played the ball, or it has come off his person, he must not touch it unless in defence of his wicket. Unless a member of the fielding side gives permission for the striker to pick the ball up, he must not touch it. John Holder: In 1989 at the first Test between Pakistan and India in Karachi, there was an extraordinary incident like this one. With the match petering out to a tame draw, Salim Malik of Pakistan played a ball defensively on the off side and it stopped dead a yard away. He then used his bat to nudge the ball to the gully fielder. India's wicketkeeper, Kiran More, ran up to the wicket and said something in Urdu to Malik. Whatever it was it incensed Malik who chased after More with his bat aloft in a threatening manner. My colleague John Hampshire and I intervened and calmed things down – but if an Indian player had appealed, Malik would have been given out.

2) Give the batsman out. As the ball didn't actually strike the helmet itself, it is still live and the catch is legitimate.

3) Yes, he's out stumped. The appeal 'How's that?' covers all types of dismissals. The fact that 'over,' had been called does not prevent the stumping from being given.

3

A batsman swipes at a spin ball, and appears to edge it. The keeper takes it and appeals for a catch – then, to make sure, whips the bails off too and appeals for a stumping. You're standing at the bowler's end and refuse the catch appeal, and call 'over'. But split seconds later, your colleague at square leg gives the batsman out stumped. Is the batsman out?

Sir Jack Hobbs

Full name: John Berry Hobbs
Date of birth: December 16, 1882
Major teams: England, Surrey

Tests: 61
Ave: 56.94
Centuries: 15
Fifties: 28
High score: 211

Jack Hobbs, known as 'The Master', has a claim to being one of the greatest batsmen of all time. His 61,760 first-class runs and 199 first-class centuries are more than any other player and will, almost certainly, remain so. For Surrey, he reached 1,000 runs in a county season on 26 separate occasions, a stat that illustrates well his extraordinary longevity and consistency. In Test cricket, he scored 15 centuries and averaged 56.94 at the top of the order, where Sunil Gavaskar is his only realistic rival for the greatest-ever opener. For England he formed a famous opening partnership with Herbert Sutcliffe, himself one of the game's greats, and together they made 11 century partnerships against Australia.

As a boy Hobbs learned to play with a cricket stump as a bat, a practice that forced him to keep the bat straight and to appreciate the importance of timing. His father once stressed the importance of standing up to the wicket, and so the fundamentals of one of the greatest techniques was formed: playing impeccably straight, standing up and timing sweetly. It served him well: he was equally capable on all surfaces and against all types of bowling. His status in world cricket was confirmed when he was voted one of the five Wisden Cricketers of the Twentieth Century. He died in 1963.

Geoff Boycott

Full name: Geoffrey Boycott
Date of birth: October 21, 1940
Teams: England, Yorkshire

Tests: 108		ODIs: 36	
Ave: 47.72		Ave: 36.06	
Centuries: 22		Centuries: 1	
Fifties: 42		Fifties: 9	
High score: 246*		High score: 105	

Geoffrey Boycott has become shorthand for a certain type of player: dour, selfish, and never one to give up his wicket on behalf of a team-mate. Such a reputation, however, doesn't do him justice. Boycott was an opener with an average nearing 50 during an era, as he likes to remind people, of uncovered pitches and fearsome fast bowlers. He's co-holder of the record for the most Test centuries for England (with Wally Hammond and Colin Cowdrey), and his importance to his team was illustrated by the fact that England lost only 20 of the matches that he played in.

Boycott's mandate was to see off the new ball, which he excelled at thanks to the compactness of his technique, his aversion to hitting the ball in the air, and his fine square-cuts and on-drives. If he hadn't missed 30 Tests between 1974 and '77, Boycott would almost certainly have broken many of his country's batting records and, quite possibly, captained England. The self-imposed exile did, however, lead to his finest moment: scoring 107 and 80 not out in his comeback Test at Trent Bridge against the Aussies. Since retirement, Boycott has become a fixture in the commentary box – a famously highly opinionated but perceptive expert on the game.

1 A batsman runs a sharp single and just manages to get home as all three stumps are spreadeagled in an attempted run-out. The ball ricochets away and the batsmen set off and complete another run. With no wicket to throw the ball at, the fielding side insist the ball was dead after the wicket collapsed. The second run should not be allowed. What is your decision?

1 A fielder, stooping to stop a fast-moving ball, stubs his finger and cries out in pain. The batsman at the striker's end, who'd started to run for a quick single, thinks the noise is his partner calling 'no', so stops and tries to return to his crease. But the fielder, despite his pain, manages to hurl the ball at his wicket and appeals. What is your decision?

Answers

1) Out. Obstruction can be physical or verbal, but must be deliberate. In this instance, the fielder genuinely cried out in pain and, on appeal, the batsman is out. You can ask the fielding captain if he really wants the appeal to stand in the circumstances, but if he says yes, the appeal must be upheld.

2) Yes, award four runs. If, in fielding, the ball or any part of the fielder's person touches or is grounded beyond the boundary fence, rope or line, with the ball in his hand or touching his person, a boundary is scored.

3) Not out. The bowler cannot bowl until the striker is ready, and you must make sure this is the case. There is no stipulation as to where the bowler can start his run from, though, so it's up to you to make sure there is no sharp practice or gamesmanship. **John Holder:** I recall an incident from my playing days with Hampshire when we were playing Northants at Northampton, with the home team batting. Sarfraz Nawaz, 6ft 3in, was facing our fast bowler Bob Cottam, also 6ft 3in, bowling around the wicket. Tom Spencer, the umpire at the bowler's end, stood only 5ft 3in tall, but Sarfraz still claimed he couldn't see Cottam as he ran in to bowl. Tom told him in no uncertain terms to stop wasting everyone's time.

28

2

The side batting need two runs for a win, with one ball left to be bowled. The fast bowler puts everything into his delivery, but you signal a wide. The batsmen set off to complete what they believe is the winning run. What is your decision?

3

A spin bowler, attempting to bowl an off-break, loses his grip and the ball slips out of his hand. A fielder picks it up and lobs it back to the bowler. The batsman protests, insisting he had the right to hit the ball. What is your decision?

Answers

1) You would allow the run to stand. With the ball 'live', if the wicket is broken, a member of the fielding side can remake it and, with the runner out of his ground, run him out. The fact that the stumps are lying flat does not cause the ball to be 'dead'.

2) If a wide is bowled and the keeper misses it you would allow the run to stand. John Holder: Many years ago at Taunton, Nixon Mclean of Hampshire bowled three successive balls to Piran Holloway of Somerset that flew past first slip to the boundary. I signalled wide for each and, as the penalty then was two runs for a wide and they all went to the boundary, it added 18 wides to Somerset's total.

3) You would call 'no ball', then 'dead ball' and the striker has no right to hit it. Before the laws were rewritten (in 2000), the striker was allowed one attempt to strike the ball.

Ryan Sidebottom

Full name: Ryan Jay Sidebottom
Date of birth: January 15, 1978
Teams: England, Nottinghamshire, Yorkshire

Tests: 18	ODIs: 16
Ave: 15.64	Ave: 10.20
Wickets: 76	Wickets: 24
Bowling ave: 25.68	Bowling ave: 27.54
BBI: 7-47	BBM: 3-19
BBM: 10-139	

Sidebottom's success on the international stage was hailed as the triumph of the journeyman, as proof of the benefits of 'learning your trade'. Red-faced, with long hair streaming behind, he runs in as if he's about to unleash a missile – only to reveal a style based on accuracy, intelligence and the ability to swing the ball both ways. His left-arm fast-medium is particularly effective around the wicket.

The son of Arnie Sidebottom – Manchester United defender and one-Test wonder – Ryan appeared, after a wicketless performance against Pakistan in 2001, to be destined for a Test career as lengthy as his father's. But after a surprise recall against West Indies in 2007, he proved a revelation: he took eight wickets in the match, 16 in the three-match series, and went on to be voted England's player of the year. In just a matter of months Sidebottom had gone from the international wilderness to being the mainstay of England's reconfigured bowling attack. Persistent back problems, however, raised the possibility that his international career may be as brief as it has been admirable.

2

In light rain a fielder races to stop a ball crossing the boundary. He reaches it in time, but slips as he tries to retrieve it. As he falls on the ball one of his feet is touching the boundary rope – but neither his hand or arm touched the ball, which was stationary. Do you signal four?

3

A slow bowler bowling around the wicket with a very short approach decides to vary his routine. Taking no run whatsoever, he walks behind you, so the batsman can't see him, then suddenly steps out and releases the ball. The batsman, unprepared, is bowled. What is your decision?

Wally Hammond

Full name:
Walter Reginald
Hammond
Date of birth:
June 19, 1903
Major teams:
England,
Gloucestershire

Tests: 85
Ave: 58.45
Centuries: 22
Fifties: 24
High score: 336*
Wickets: 83
Bowling ave: 37.80
BBI: 5-36 BBM: 7-87

1 You're the more experienced umpire, working for the first time with a young colleague. In the second innings your colleague gives a batsman out without an appeal. The batsman protests and refuses to walk. Is he correct?

2 The on-strike batsman hits the ball and decides to run a quick single. As he reaches the non-striking end the ball is thrown straight at that wicket but, before reaching it, the batsman hits the wicket sliding his bat in and knocks the bails off. What do you give?

TREVILLION.

Wally Hammond belongs in the very highest echelon of batsmen, worthy of standing alongside Donald Bradman and WG Grace. A classical back-foot batsman with a powerful drive and a watertight defence, Hammond has stats that bear comparison with any player in the history of the game: joint most Test centuries for England; a Test average of 58.45; the highest average of those who have passed 50,000 first-class runs; and the third most first-class centuries of all-time. He was also a world-class fielder and, as evidenced by 732 first-class wickets at 30.58, could have

been a top all-rounder if he hadn't been so dedicated to his batting.

Hammond's reputation was enhanced by his appearance and character: aloof, quiet, powerful and almost regal, he intimidated opponents in a manner later perfected by Viv Richards. This same aloofness, however, led to an often complicated personal life. Hammond also had the misfortune to play in the era of Bradman, who often overshadowed the Englishman: at any other point in history Hammond would have been the world's pre-eminent batsman. He died in 1965.

James Anderson

Full name: James
Michael Anderson
Date of birth:
30 July, 1982
Major teams: England,
Lancashire

Tests: 29
Ave: 13.66
Wickets: 104
Bowling ave: 34.51
BBI: 7-43 BBM: 9-98

ODIs: 101
Wickets: 127
Bowling ave: 31.62
BBM: 4/23

1 A slow bowler in his delivery stride notices the batsman backing up is well out of his crease. He does not release the ball and instead whips off the bails and appeals for a run-out. What is your decision?

3

A batsman, in trying to avoid being hit by a bouncer, removes one hand from the bat and puts it in front of his face. The ball flicks his glove and is caught by the wicketkeeper. What is your decision?

Answers

1) The batsman is right to protest and should be given not out. There is no such thing as a senior umpire. Although one may be more experienced, they both have equal authority. In this case, according to the laws, there must be an appeal before a batsman can be given out. So take your colleague to one side and remind him of the law – the batsman would be allowed to remain at the wicket.

2) Not out on appeal. Since the bat broke the wicket before the ball, the batsman was clearly in and, as long as there is no indication that he broke the wicket deliberately to prevent the ball breaking it, he cannot be given out for obstruction.

3) Not out. He cannot be given out caught if the hand that was struck wasn't holding the bat. In a Test match at Headingley in the late Eighties, with Pakistan bowling in England's second innings, Imran Khan bowled a fast, sharply rising delivery from the Kirkstall Lane end to Chris Broad. Broad pulled his bottom hand off the bat as the ball bounced and it went on to flick his glove. It was caught by the wicketkeeper and umpire David Shepherd gave Broad out, because he thought the hand was still on the bat. Tim Robinson, the non-striker, said that from where he was the decision looked correct. However, the camera square on the off legsidside revealed that the ball had struck the hand off the bat and therefore he should have been not out.

James Anderson burst onto the international scene aged just 20, when he enjoyed a fantastic VB Series and 2003 World Cup. In that tournament he destroyed Pakistan and, though he was chastened by Australia, it appeared to be the beginning of glorious England career. A five-wicket haul in his debut Test and a hat-trick against South Africa followed, but then deficiencies in his technique – and perhaps in his termperament – were revealed. After a series of bad performances he was forced into a period of rehabilitation. A lengthy period on the sidelines followed and comebacks were curtailed by injuries. However, by 2008 he had recaptured his best form and, with it, his Test place. For much of the season he shouldered the burden of being the senior bowler.

Athletic and lithe, Anderson bowls with genuine pace and posseses the ability to swing the bowl prodigiously. The flaw that has blighted his career, however, is an occasional waywardness and the tendency to follow a monumental performance with a below-par display. He is also a fine fielder – fast and agile – with an excellent arm.

2

A fielder racing to stop a ball from reaching the boundary swoops to pick it up and appears to fail to collect it. The two batsmen take advantage of the misfield and go for a second run, but the fielder turns and throws the ball in. It wasn't a misfield, but a deliberate attempt to mislead the batsmen. With the batsman out of his crease the keeper whips off the bails and appeals. What is your decision?

TREVILLION

3

Two fielders run to catch a high, dropping ball and almost collide as both manage to get one of their hands on the ball. Somehow the ball is not spilled and together they complete the catch. The batsman claims he is not out, insisting that only one fielder can catch a ball. What do you do?

Answers

1) Not out on appeal. Once the bowler is in his delivery stride he cannot run the non-striker out, even if he's out of his ground; it can, however, be attempted during the run-up before the delivery stride. John Holder: Before the laws were rewritten in 2000, the bowler could run out the non-striker in his delivery stride. A former India player, Vinoo Mankad, was well known for this practice and batsmen dismissed in this manner were said to have been 'Mankaded'. It created scenes of players accusing one another of cheating and unsporting behaviour, so the law was changed.

2) The batsman is out. John Holder: The fact that the fielder duped him is hard luck, but batsmen tend to know from experience when an opponent is trying to fool them and usually hold to the common saying in cricket that you never run on a misfield – Dermot Reeve regularly tried this ploy on batsmen, but I never saw him succeed.

3) The batsman is out, caught, on appeal. John Holder: This is an unlikely scenario, but as we all know in cricket the unlikely does happen. In this case, as long as the ball has not touched the ground, the wicket stands. However, the catch can only be attributed to one fielder – it doesn't matter which one – but the two must decide between themselves who claims the catch.

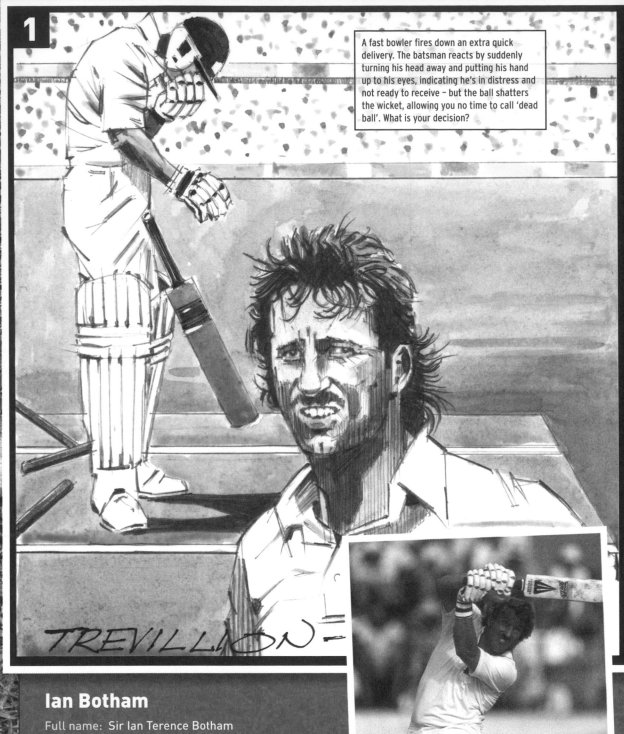

1

A fast bowler fires down an extra quick delivery. The batsman reacts by suddenly turning his head away and putting his hand up to his eyes, indicating he's in distress and not ready to receive – but the ball shatters the wicket, allowing you no time to call 'dead ball'. What is your decision?

TREVILLION

Ian Botham

Full name: Sir Ian Terence Botham
Date of birth: November 24, 1955
Teams: England, Somerset, Worcestershire, Durham

Tests: 102	ODIs: 116
Ave: 33.54	Ave: 23.21
Centuries: 14	Centuries: 0
Fifties: 22	Fifties: 9
High score: 208	High score: 79
Wickets: 383	Wickets: 145
Bowling ave: 28.40	Bowling ave: 28.54
BBI: 8-34 BBM: 13-106	BBM: 4-31

2

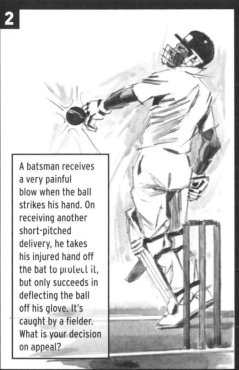

A batsman receives a very painful blow when the ball strikes his hand. On receiving another short-pitched delivery, he takes his injured hand off the bat to protect it, but only succeeds in deflecting the ball off his glove. It's caught by a fielder. What is your decision on appeal?

3

A fielder at first slip takes a very low catch and appeals – the batsman walks without waiting for your signal. The new batsman is taking his guard when the fielder who took the catch approaches you and admits the ball touched the ground first. He asks you to recall the batsman, who is now in the pavilion. What do you do?

Answers

1) The bowler's end umpire has to be absolutely convinced in his mind that there was no act of gamesmanship on the batsman's behalf and that he was, at that moment, genuinely inconvenienced in some way or other. You then call and signal 'dead ball'.

2) Not out. A batsman struck on the hand by a legal delivery can only be out caught if the hand is holding, or in contact with, the bat when struck by the ball.

3) If a batsman leaves the wicket under a misapprehension, thinking he's been dismissed when he hasn't, you can call him back – but it must be before he has crossed the boundary line. During a game at Headingley in a C&G match between Yorkshire and Derbyshire, I gave Ant Botha of Derby out lbw, but then realised from the sound that the ball had struck the bat first. I revoked the signal and called Botha back. He was three-quarters of the way off the field at the time. He said thank you to me afterwards about six times.

Ian Botham was one of the game's great all-rounders, becoming the first player to score both 5,000 runs and take 300 wickets in Test cricket. As a hard-hitting batsman he invariably attacked, resulting in an unpredictability demonstrated by the figures – 14 ducks and 14 centuries. His fast-medium bowling appeared to lack finesse but he still managed to collect 383 Test wickets, the most by an England player. With both disciplines he seemed to rely on inspiration: the off-days more than compensated for by days of match-winning brilliance.

Beefy's golden hour was undoubtedly the 1981 Ashes, dubbed 'Botham's Ashes'. His captaincy having proved disastrous, with no victories from 12 matches, he quit after the second Ashes Test and rediscovered the freedom that made him great. In the subsequent three Tests he scored two bravado centuries and bowled beautifully, including a spell of five wickets for one run.

One mystery was his one day international record. An attacking all-rounder, Botham should have revelled in the licence afforded by the shortened game, but managed a batting average of only 23.21 with no centuries.

Regardless, Botham's heroics helped rejuvenate cricket in England and established him as one of the game's legendary matchwinners.

Richie Benaud

Full name: Richard Benaud
Date of birth: October 6, 1930
Major teams: Australia, New South Wales

Tests: 63	High score: 122
Ave: 24.45	Wickets: 248
Centuries: 3	Bowling ave: 27.03
Fifties: 9	BBI: 7-72 BBM: 11-105

1 It's the last ball of a one-day innings, the scores are tied and the striker digs out a yorker. His partner, who is well advanced down the pitch, backing up, calls for a single. However the ball spins back towards the stumps and the non-striker, as he dives in to complete the single, knocks the ball away with his bat. What is your decision?

2 In a minor counties match, your colleague is injured by a ball and is unable to continue. Both captains want the match to carry on with you as the sole umpire. Can you allow this?

TREVILLON -

Brian Lara

Full name: Brian Charles Lara
Date of birth: May 2, 1969
Major teams: West Indies, Trinidad & Tobago, Warwickshire

Tests: 131	ODIs: 299
Ave: 52.88	Centuries: 19
Centuries: 34	Fifties: 63
Fifties: 48	High score: 169
High score: 400*	

1 In the closing stages of a match a fast bowler, who dives in attempting a return catch, damages the shoulder of his bowling arm on landing. He asks if he can complete his over underarm. What is your decision?

Answers

1) The bowler cannot complete the over underarm. The law forbids this, so another player, who didn't bowl the previous over or isn't due to bowl the next one, will have to bowl the remaining ball. At the end of a one-day international between Australia and New Zealand in 1981, the Aussie captain, Greg Chappell, instructed his younger brother, Trevor, to bowl the last ball underarm – to make the delivery difficult to score the six runs needed for victory. Australia duly won, but the incident caused a furore. Although it was legal at the time, it was regarded as a glaring example of unsporting behaviour. The laws were rewritten in 2000 to outlaw underarm bowling.

2) Both umpires, with the scorers, must go through the scorebook to correct the mistake. Scorers are asked by umpires before the start of the match to cross-check regularly to avoid errors. Ultimately the umpires are responsible for the scores – in club cricket many keep a record as the game goes on.

3) The striker is out – caught. Once the appeal is made, you must react to the first incident, in this case the catch. The ball becomes dead as soon as a batsman is dismissed, so the fielding side can neither specify which batsman they wish to be dismissed in a situation like this, or get both batsmen out on one ball.

To later generations of cricket fans, Richie Benaud is a cricket journalist and broadcaster of huge authority and accuracy. But in his younger days he was a Test-class all-rounder: a tricky, thinking leg-spinner, an athletic fielder, and an energetic lower-order batman. His initial years in the Australia side were disappointing but, despite his struggle with both bat and ball, the selectors persisted. The turning point was the 1957-58 tour to South Africa, where Benaud scored two centuries and took 30 wickets. From then on, his bowling became more prominent and he formed a famous partnership with fellow all-rounder Alan Davidson.

Appointed Australia captain in 1958, he made use of the talents that he would later bring to his journalism: calmness, great powers of communication and a deep, intuitive understanding of tactics. Under his leadership, Australia won back the Ashes in 1959, the first time since 1951, and he retained them twice. He advocated positive, attacking cricket – which the Australia team have stuck to ever since. Since retiring his media work has made him one of the most respected figures in the sport.

3 The new batsman takes a right-hand guard, but after four deliveries in the over, he asks the umpire to give him middle and leg for a left-hand guard and prepares to face. Do you allow it? If so can he continue to do it throughout the innings?

Answers

1) Give the batsman out. If the non-striker, in diving in to make his ground, has deflected the ball away and you judge it to have been obstruction, he's out. Obstruction is always seen as deliberate and you must give the wicket.

2) Yes, you can continue the match. If no other qualified umpire is available, a spectator or player not batting can umpire at square leg for both ends and you would officiate at the bowling ends. John Holder: At Colchester several years ago, Nigel Cowley had to leave the field during a county match and George Clark, a former league umpire in Essex, took over the duties at square leg for the rest of the day.

3) Yes, allow it. It's not against the law for a striker to change stance between the balls. You cannot prevent it and the fact that he has informed you changes off and leg side. He can continue to do this throughout the innings but if it results in play being held up, you can warn him for time-wasting, for which penalty runs may be awarded to the fielding side.

No batsman has ever matched Lara's capacity for building monumental scores. His 400 not out, made against England at St John's in 2004, remains the highest score ever made in a Test; his 375, scored against the same opponents at the same ground a decade before, is the third.

His 501 not out for Warwickshire against Durham in 1994 is a first-class record. His tally of nine Test double hundreds is bettered only by Bradman's 12 and, together with Bradman and Virender Sehwag, he has scored a record two triple centuries.

West Indies, still dominant when Lara made his debut, declined so fast that by the time he reached his pomp 'The Prince' often seemed to be batting in a one man team. Against Sri Lanka in 2001-02 he scored 42% of his side's runs. In his two spells as captain he had the misfortune to preside over a fading and ill-disciplined team, though the suspicion remains that he was simply poorly suited to the task: too brilliant an individual to be an effective leader of lesser men.

2	50	for	4
	extras		8
	overs		48
last man	JOHNS		25

7	2	
11	7	
2	1	
10	19	
	4	39 5
8		9

At lunch the two scorers disagree over the score. What do you do?

3 A spin bowler taking a clean one-handed return catch off a tail-end batsman doesn't appeal but, instead, in the same movement, throws down the wicket of the opening batsman (who is backing up and out of his crease) and appeals for a run-out. What is your decision?

TREVILLION

35

Viv Richards

Full name: Sir Isaac Vivian Alexander Richards
Date of birth: March 7, 1952
Teams: West Indies, Combined Islands, Somerset, Leeward Islands, Queensland, Glamorgan

Tests: 121	ODIs: 187
Ave: 50.23	Ave: 47.00
Centuries: 24	Centuries: 11
Fifties: 45	Fifties: 45
High score: 291	High score: 189*
Wickets: 32	Wickets: 118
Bowling ave: 61.37	Bowling ave: 35.83

Such was his reputation and aura – with his swagger, his gum, and always without a helmet – that Richards often beat bowlers simply by turning up. Sir Viv was one of the greatest players of all time: a batsmen of unparalleled aggression, a world-class fielder and a more than handy off-spin bowler. He always looked to dominate – which was sometimes his undoing early on in an innings. But his sharp eyes and brilliant hand-eye coordination usually ensured that he was in long enough to do the damage.

Richards played predominantly on the front foot, flicking the ball to leg or creaming it through extra-cover, but he was equally adept at hooking and pulling and even, if the whim took him, of playing defensively. He was also a fine captain, and in his 11 years as skipper he never lost a series – the only West Indian to have achieved such a feat. Many feel his batting was second only to Donald Bradman's, and he has been voted one of Wisden's Five Cricketers of the Twentieth century and the greatest ever ODI batsman.

1 With the light fading fast, the fielding side are desperately pressing for a victory, but the incoming batsman takes an unusually long time coming to the wicket. A frustrated fielder appeals and demands he should be given out. What is your decision?

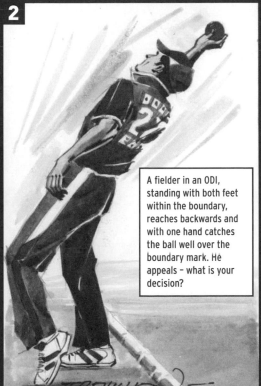

2

A fielder in an ODI, standing with both feet within the boundary, reaches backwards and with one hand catches the ball well over the boundary mark. He appeals – what is your decision?

3

A batsman advances down the wicket and is beaten by the spin. The keeper collects the ball in front of the stumps, removes the bails and appeals. The batsman stands his ground and insists he is not out. What is your decision?

Answers

1) On appeal, if he has taken more than three minutes, you would give him out – 'timed out'. The incoming batsman has this time from the fall of a wicket for him, or his partner, to take strike.

2) Give the batsman out. As long as no part of the fielder's person touches the boundary fence, board or marking, or is grounded beyond it, the catch is legal.

3) Call 'no ball' and give the batsman not out, since the striker cannot be stumped off a no ball. The wicketkeeper cannot catch the ball in front of the stumps unless the striker has hit it or it has come off his person.

Matthew Hoggard

Full name: Matthew James Hoggard
Date of birth: December 31, 1976
Teams: England, Yorkshire

Tests: 67
Ave: 7.27
Wickets: 248
Bowling ave: 30.50
BBI: 7-61 BBM: 12-205
ODIs: 26
Ave: 4.25
Wickets: 32
Bowling ave: 36.00
BBM: 5-49

Matthew Hoggard always maintained that his bowling is all about 'closing my eyes and wanging the ball down'. If so, he wanged in style, and produced near-perfect examples of English swing bowling. Such self-deprecation ensured that his name was often preceded by such terms as 'yeoman' and 'faithful' and it stopped him from gaining the recognition that he deserved. From the famous Ashes quartet, Freddie Flintoff was more heroic, Steve Harmison and Simon Jones were both faster, but none was more successful, in the long run, than Hoggard. With 248 Test wickets he currently stands sixth in England's all-time wicket takers.

He focused on line and length, moving the ball away, but without any real pace he could be nullified if conditions weren't right for swing. This occasional hittability meant he made only 26 ODI appearances. In Tests, though, he was a vital component of the England team. Highlights included a series-winning 12-wicket haul against South Africa in 2004 and a rare cover drive that won the Trent Bridge Test in 2005 and set up an Ashes victory. His pace gradually decreased, though: in 2007 he was dropped, harshly, and his international future was threatened by a crop of younger bowlers.

1

A batsman sways out of the way of a bouncer, but isn't quite quick enough. The ball strikes his helmet and races off over the boundary. You signal four runs, but the fielding side angrily point out that the batsman didn't attempt a shot. What do you do?

Answers

1) Do nothing – you were right: this is four leg-byes. The law allows the awarding of leg-byes where a batsman, in trying to avoid being hit by a delivery, takes evasive action but the ball strikes any part of his person. If the ball goes over the boundary you award four runs, or if it stops short, the batsmen can run. In the latter case a run-out can also be effected.

2) Not out. The bowler's end umpire must decide whether or not the batsman's action was deliberate, and in this case it was purely accidental: there will be no penalty for obstruction against the batsman.

3) No – award four runs. Part of your job is to get to the ground 45 minutes before play is scheduled to start: there are various pre-match duties to perform. One of them is to inform both captains about any obstacles on the field of play and, that if any spectators or animals come on and make contact with the ball while it is in play, you will award a boundary. This means you can avoid any potentially embarrassing confusions like this when the ball is caught. John Holder: In my early years, umpiring a county second-XI match, a dog ran on to the field, avoiding everyone's attempts to catch it. My colleague and I immediately called and signalled dead ball to avoid getting into a situation like this one.

1

The heavens open and the players are forced to leave the field. Two hours later the pitch and surrounding area are playable, but the outfield near the boundary is still very wet. The fielding captain insists they want to play and tells you he will take responsibility for his players. What is your response?

Answers

1) The umpires are the final judges when it comes to the fitness of the ground. If, in your opinion, conditions are so dangerous that there's a risk of injury to players or umpires, do not allow play to start or continue.

2) If they appeal, and you confirm the light is still the same as when you first judged it unfit, you must grant the batsmen's wishes. They cannot just walk off, though, without making a formal appeal to you first. John Holder: In my first Test match, in 1988 at Lord's, between England and Sri Lanka, with England batting, Allan Lamb and Robin Smith were at the wicket in the afternoon when the light began to deteriorate. My colleague David Constant and I conferred and offered the light to the batsmen, who refused. Within half an hour it was almost pitch black and the batsmen finally appealed, which we accepted. As we were walking off, Lamb, forever the joker, said: 'It wasn't that I couldn't see the ball. I couldn't see John Holder at square-leg. All I can see is a ghostly white coat.'

3) Yes, stop the game. If the light is as bad as this there's serious risk that someone will be struck, be it players or umpires. You have a duty of care to all involved.

2

A batsman, desperate not to be run out, dives towards his crease, but falls short. As he hits the ground, he loses his grip on his bat. It flies out of his hand and hits the fielder's leg just as he's about to run him out. The pain causes the fielder to drop the ball and the batsman scrambles back into the crease. What is your decision?

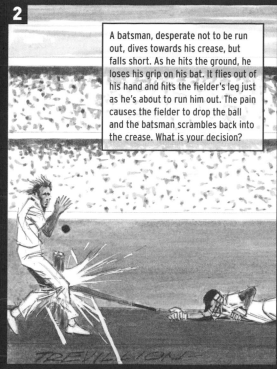

3

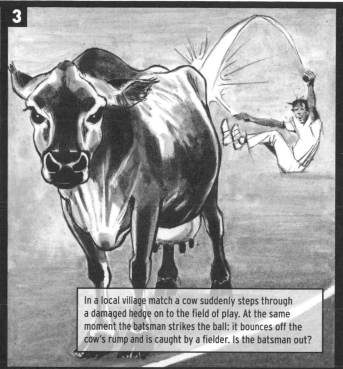

In a local village match a cow suddenly steps through a damaged hedge on to the field of play. At the same moment the batsman strikes the ball: it bounces off the cow's rump and is caught by a fielder. Is the batsman out?

Andrew Strauss

Full name: Andrew John Strauss
Date of birth: March 2, 1977
Teams: England, Middlesex

Tests: 53	ODIs: 78	
Ave: 41.07	Ave: 31.98	
Centuries: 12	Centuries: 2	
Fifties: 14	Fifties: 14	
High score: 177	High score: 152	

For the first two years of Andrew Strauss's Test career, his progress was seamless. Having scored 112 and 83 on his debut, he went on to score 1,323 runs at an average of over 55 in his first year. Against Australia in 2005 he hit two centuries, the only player on either side to reach three figures twice. But then a dip, exacerbated by some unlucky umpiring decisions and the loss of the stand-in captaincy, degenerated into a prolonged loss of form. Having scored 10 centuries in his first 30 Tests he then failed to score a ton in his next 15. He was dropped for the tour of Sri Lanka in 2007 but, recalled against New Zealand, went on to hit an ugly, slow but career-saving 177 in the third match.

After his recall he modified his style, becoming even more conservative. It made him less dangerous but more reliable – making him the obvious choice as captain to steady the ship when Kevin Pietersen resigned in January 2009.

2

You offer the light to the batsmen. They decline and decide to play on, but halfway through the next over they have a rethink and, although the light has not deteriorated, they want to walk off. What is your decision?

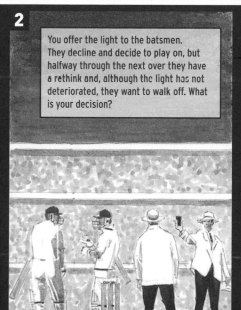

3

It's another dark, wet day. You offer the light to both captains, but to your surprise they decide to play on. It's so gloomy that you fail to see the very next ball and are nearly decapitated. Can you overrule the captains and stop play for the safety of the umpires?

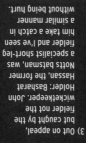

Tea is scheduled for 3.30pm, but at 3.33pm the ninth wicket falls on the last ball of the over. Do you allow play to continue or take tea at the allotted time?

A slip fielder realises the ball is going over his head, so he takes his cap off, uses it to knock the ball down, takes the catch in his other hand and appeals. What do you give?

Answers

1) Allow play to continue. If nine wickets are down at the agreed time for the tea interval, play continues for 30 minutes or the innings ends.

2) Not out. Using his cap in this manner is illegal fielding. So call and signal dead ball, award five penalty runs to the batting side and report the fielder to the authorities.

3) Out on appeal, but caught by the fielder not the wicketkeeper, John Hassan, the former Notts batsman, was a specialist short-leg fielder and I've seen him take a catch in a similar manner without being hurt.

Lasith Malinga

Full name: Separamadu Lasith Malinga
Date of birth: August 28, 1983
Teams: Sri Lanka, Galle, Nondescripts, Kent

Tests: 28
Ave: 9.14
Wickets: 91
Bowling ave: 33.80
BBI: 5-68 BBM: 9-210

ODIs: 53
Ave: 6.57
Wickets: 79
Bowling ave: 25.58
BBM: 4-44

Lasith Malinga, or 'Malinga the slinga', has an action unique in modern cricket: he bowls almost round-arm, producing a rapid, slinging delivery that, plenty of batsmen have confirmed, is incredibly hard to pick up, given the uncomfortable angle of delivery. He developed the bizarre technique by learning the

sport using a tennis ball in his village's coconut groves – the result was his only successful delivery being a fast yorker. As a youngster he was spotted and invited to join Sri Lanka's Cricket Foundation and, despite his rawness, he took eight wickets in his first game with Galle CC, after only five games with a leather ball. He was soon promoted to the Sri Lanka Test side and marked his debut with the wickets of Australia's Adam Gilchrist and Darren Lehmann.

Though erratic, he immediately cemented his position in both the Test and one-day sides. But it was the 2007 World Cup that really made his name: he took four wickets in four balls against South Africa – the first time that had happened in international cricket – and picked up 18 wickets in all. His success in Tests, however, has been patchy, perhaps the result of an action that, though potentially devastating, makes control very difficult.

A slow bowler beats the bat but the ball, which hits the wicket, doesn't dislodge the bails. The batsman is delighted to still be in and you signal 'over'. Only then does one of the bails drop. The wicketkeeper appeals, but the batsman insists he's still in because the over had been called. What is your decision?

With the last ball of the over, a quick bowler delivers a terrifyingly fast, vicious beamer. You have no doubt it was intentional, so you tell him he's banned from bowling for the rest of the innings. Immediately you are surrounded by the entire fielding team who protest loudly. What action do you take to defuse the situation?

3

A batsman strikes a ball and it hits a close fielder in the midriff. The fielder doubles up in pain and falls to the ground. But the ball is still lodged against him and hasn't touched the ground. The wicketkeeper picks the ball up and claims the catch. What is your decision?

K.S. Ranjitsinhji

Full name: Kumar Shri Ranjitsinhji (Ranjitsinhji Vibhaji Jadeja, Maharaja Jam Sahib of Nawanagar)
(Colonel His Highness Shri Sir Ranjitsinhji Vibhaji, Maharajah Jam Sahib of Nawanagar)
Date of birth: September 10, 1872
Major teams: England, Sussex

Tests: 15   Fifties: 6
Ave: 44.95   High score: 175
Centuries: 2

K.S Ranjitsinhji, who died in 1933, was part of the golden age of cricket, an era that produced the likes of CB Fry, Gilbert Jessop and Victor Trumper. It was during this period, from 1890 to the First World War, that that modern techniques were perfected and Test cricket blossomed. No one, arguably, contributed more to the period than Prince Ranji. Crowds flocked to see a player reputed to be among the most entertaining to have played the game.

Ranji was an extraordinarily stylish batsman. He perfected the cut-stroke and invented the leg-glance, while his virtuosity and mobility helped break the assumption that front-foot play was a necessity. However, for

all his elegance he didn't lack substance. In 1900 he scored over 3,000 runs at an average of 87.57 and hit five double centuries. Three times in his career he hit over 1,000 runs in a calendar month. In total he scored nearly 25,000 first-class runs at average of 56.37.

Adopted by England, he scored a Test century on his debut and then proceeded to replicate his successful opening partnership, honed at Sussex, with his great friend CB Fry. Although many considered his batting magical, he himself thought it a simple practice; his dictum being: 'First, see where the ball is going to pitch, then go to it; then it hit it.'

3

Two lightning-fast fielders, running to make the same catch, realise that the high flying ball will sail over the boundary for six. They react quickly, and one fielder lifts his team-mate high in the air to catch the ball. Both appeal. What is your decision?

1) **Not out.** John Holder: The law does not specify a time limit on how long the umpire must wait to see if a ball falls off. You must use your own judgment; I'd say this was not out.

2) **Instruct the captain to take control of his players.** He is responsible for their behaviour and would be expected to put an end to the squabbling and dissent. Both umpires would submit written reports to that team's authorities and the game's governing body outlining what had happened and whether or not the captain had done as instructed. They would convene a hearing and decide what action to take. At international level there's a referee at every match who has the power to impose immediate fines and/or suspensions in cases of dissent or bad behaviour, which has made incidents like this very rare. John Holder: In the early 1990s in a county match, I was umpiring when a fired-up Courtney Walsh of Gloucestershire overstepped the crease by some 18 inches and delivered a beamer at Peter Bowler of Derbyshire. It whistled past his head, bounced awkwardly and nearly decapitated wicketkeeper Jack Russell. I called 'no ball' and warned Walsh. I had no doubt the beamer was intentional, but until the law change in 2000 you couldn't ban the offender.

3) Although this is an unlikely scenario, if the fielder did catch the ball the striker would be out.

1

A fast bowler, who has already been no-balled twice, comes roaring in but again oversteps the popping crease. You call 'no ball' but the bowler keeps hold of the ball and doesn't release it. What action do you take?

TREVILLION —

2

The two captains meet for the toss before a match. The home captain spins the coin but the away captain waits until it has hit the ground and then calls. The home captain insists he must call while the coin is in the air and that the toss should be repeated. Is he right?

Answers

1) If the bowler doesn't release the ball it doesn't count in that over. In this case, having already called 'no ball' because the bowler did not actually release it, you would revoke your signal and no run will be awarded to the batting side.

2) Yes, the call must be made while the coin is in the air. This prevents any chance of gamesmanship, so the toss should be repeated.

3) Yes, if both captains and umpires agree, the pitch can be switched if the original is proving to be dangerous.

England Lead by 415 with Four Wickets Yet to Fall

JARDINE MAKING SURE OF VICTORY

ENGLAND.—First innings.
D. R. Jardine b Wall..................... 24
Sutcliffe c Wall b O'Reilly............ 9
Hammond c Oldfield b Wall........... 2
Ames b Ironmonger..................... 3
Leyland b O'Reilly...................... 42
R. E. S. Wyatt c Richardson b Grimmett..................... 51
Paynter c Fingleton b Wall........... 78
G. O. Allen lbw b Grimmett.......... 77
Verity c Richardson b Wall........... 15
Voce b Wall............................. 45
Larwood not out....................... 3
B 1, lb 7, nb 7....................... 15
Total..................... 341

FALL OF WICKETS.
1 2 3 4 5 6 7 8 9 10
4 16 16 30 186 196 228 324 336 341

BOWLING ANALYSIS.
England—First innings.

	Overs.	Mdns.	Runs.	Wkts.
T. W. Wall	34.1	10	72	5
W. J. O'Reilly	50	19	82	2
H. Ironmonger	20	6	50	2
C. V. Grimmett	28	6	94	2
S. J. McCabe	14	3	28	0

Wall bowled three and O'Reilly four no-balls.

AUSTRALIA.—First innings.
J. S. Fingleton c Ames b Allen........
W. M. Woodfull b Allen................ 0
D. G. Bradman c Allen b Larwood.... 13
S. J. McCabe c Jardine b Larwood.... 8
W. H. Ponsford b Voce................
V. Y. Richardson b Allen.............. 85
W. A. Oldfield retired hurt........... 23
C. V. Grimmett c Voce b Allen........ 41
T. W. Wall b Hammond................ 10
W. J. O'Reilly b Larwood............. 4
H. Ironmonger not out................ 0
B 2, lb 11, nb 1..................... 14
Total..................... 222

FALL OF WICKETS.
1 2 3 4 5 6 7 8 9 10
1 18 34 51 131 194 212 222 222

BOWLING ANALYSIS.
Larwood.... 25 . 6 . 55 . 3
G. O. Allen.... 23 . 4 . 71 . 4
Hammond.... 10 . 3 . 30 . 1
Voce.... 17.4 . 4 . 39 . 1
Verity.... 18 . 7 . 31 . 0

Voce bowled one no-ball.
ENGLAND

Wall, whose catches have been a feature of the Test matches hitherto, made another brilliant catch. Some were of the opinion that it was a bump ball, and apparently Borwick, the umpire, was also in doubt, for he consulted his colleague before giving his decision. Wyatt had batted stolidly this morning while adding two to his overnight score. Altogether his innings lasted two hours thirteen minutes, and was marked by some fine hitting on the leg side yesterday. He hit four boundaries in his 49.

Allen, promoted in the batting list, partnered his captain; he played restrained cricket, and as Jardine did the same runs continued to come slowly. Jardine was at the wickets 45 minutes while adding three to his score. The first bowling change was made at 95, Ironmonger coming on for Wall. Against two slow bowlers who kept a good length and flighted the ball cleverly, run-getting was as slow as ever, but the 100 was eventually reached after the innings had lasted two hours 49 minutes.

The batsmen now became a little more enterprising, so at 112 Grimmett was put on instead of O'Reilly. His first ball—a full toss—was promptly hit to the boundary by Jardine, but soon afterwards a faster ball got Allen leg-before-wicket. This was at 123, when the partnership had put on 32 runs. Allen batted 52 minutes for his 15 and hit one boundary. Hammond came in for the few minutes remaining before lunch, and the score was carried to 130 without further loss (Jardine 46, Hammond 11).

The game was just as lifeless after lunch, when O'Reilly and Wall began the bowling. Jardine went on in his own stolid way, and Hammond was also subdued, though he did what little scoring there was, obtaining ten of the twelve runs added in 25 minutes. Ironmonger was brought on for Wall at 146,

3 A pitch is becoming too dangerous for play to continue and you're thinking about abandoning the match. But the groundsman informs you that he was preparing a wicket for another match and if he takes off its cover it will be perfect for play. Are you allowed to move the game?

Douglas Jardine

Full name: Douglas Robert Jardine
Date of birth: October 23, 1900
Major teams: England, Surrey

Tests: 22
Ave: 48.00
Centuries: 1
Fifties: 10
High score: 127

Respected in England and loathed in Australia, Douglas Jardine's reputation is still made or tarnished by his involvement in the Bodyline affair. Bodyline, as the 1932-33 Ashes series came to be known, became one of the most famous episodes in cricket history. Jardine, the England captain, formulated a plan he dubbed 'leg theory': packing the leg-side field with close catchers and bowling the ball on leg stump so that it jumped into the body of the batsman. The plan worked, with Don Bradman's average cut to 56 and England winning four of the five Tests. But it was so contentious that it sparked a diplomatic incident, with letters sent between the respective governments. Nevertheless, Jardine was unbowed, and when he himself faced leg-theory against the West Indies in 1933 he scored 127, and justified his argument that such bowling could be played if faced with sufficient bravery.

A tall, powerful batsman who revelled in defence but was strong through the leg side, Jardine was rated as one of the leading amateur batsmen of his era. While his cold, rather haughty persona alienated many and Bodyline overshadowed his achievements, Jardine, who died in 1958, still ranks as one of the most important captains in England's history.

1 A batsman, backing up, goes for a quick single but is sent back by the striker. He turns, slips and just manages to get the front end of his bat on the popping crease before the wicket is broken by the bowler. The wicketkeeper appeals, claiming part of the bat must be over the return crease, and that on the line is 'out'. What is your decision?

2 A wristy spin bowler pitches a ball just outside leg stump, which turns viciously, forcing the batsman to step back in front of his wicket to play a defensive stroke. He misses the ball, which strikes his pad, leaving him plum leg before wicket. The bowler appeals. What is your decision?

Ian Bell

Full name: Ian Ronald Bell
Date of birth: April 11, 1982
Teams: England, Warwickshire

Tests: 43	ODIs: 79
Ave: 42.36	Ave: 35.47
Centuries: 8	Centuries: 1
Fifties: 19	Fifties: 15
High score: 199	High score: 126*

Ian Bell is the only Englishman to have been dismissed in a Test on 199 – which sums up a player who hasn't consistently fulfilled his enormous talent. An elegant and compact batsman, Bell was tipped for success from an early age. When in full-flow he appears world-class but a reputation for scoring soft runs – against second-rate Test nations, in second innings – and a disappointing conversion rate of fifties to centuries has undermined his standing.

On his debut against West Indies he made 70 and the following series against Bangladesh was also very promising. But he failed comprehensively his first major examination, averaging 17.10 during the 2005 Ashes. Indeed, against the Australians, the mark against which all Englishmen are ultimately judged, he has a career average of just 25.10.

But timely reminders of his ability – centuries in three consecutive Tests against Pakistan, a fighting century against New Zealand and his 199 against South Africa – have always rescued him.

1 An opening batsman's first ball strikes him on the pads in front of his wicket. The fielding side appeal and the batsman walks off without waiting for your decision. However, you would have judged the lbw appeal not out. Can you intervene and tell the batsman he's still in?

3) He's not allowed to bowl that over – a player cannot bowl two successive overs. At the break in play both umpires make a note of who bowled the last over and from which end. They also note which batsman was facing so that on the resumption of play batsmen are at the correct ends and it's a change of bowler taking the first over. John Holder: In country cricket, some players, for a spot of fun, will test a new umpire to see how alert he is by going to the wrong end at the restart of play. This happened at Hove several years ago with Sussex playing Kent. Vanburn Holder was in his first year of umpiring and the not out overnight batsmen deliberately returned to the wrong ends. I knew what they were doing and played along, but did not allow a ball to be bowled. As the bowler got ready to run up I called dead ball from square leg, whereupon the players burst out laughing, before returning to the correct ends and restarting play. No time was lost.

3

You signal a 'no ball' which then flies head high past the batsman, forcing him to take evasive action. In doing so he steps back on to his wicket and dislodges both bails. The wicketkeeper appeals – what is your decision?

Answers

1) Give the batsman out. Part of his bat or person must ground behind the line of the popping crease to be safely 'in'. Irrespective of how wide the crease marking is, it's the back edge closest to the wicket that the bat or person needs to have crossed. John Holder: In a Twenty20 match between Durham and Yorkshire at the Riverside I called short run on two occasions because Anthony McGrath of Yorkshire had grounded the bat on top of the crease going for a second run but had failed to make sure it had crossed the back edge.

2) Not out. A striker cannot be given out lbw to a ball pitching outside the leg stump – even if it strikes him on the pad and would have gone on to hit the wicket. John Holder: Shane Warne would probably have doubled his tally of wickets had the law been different. When he bowls his leg spinners from around the wicket to right-handers, they know he cannot get a leg-before decision when the ball has pitched outside leg and so were able to pad or kick the ball away without fear of being given out lbw.

3) Not out. The only ways either batsman can be dismissed from a no ball are: run out, obstructing a fielder, handled ball or hit the ball twice.

Michael Vaughan

Full name: Michael Paul Vaughan
Date of birth: October 29, 1974
Teams: England, Yorkshire

Tests: 82		ODIs: 86	
Ave: 41.44		Ave: 27.15	
Centuries: 18		Centuries: 0	
Fifties: 18		Fifties: 16	
High score: 197		High score: 90*	

A classical top-order batsman, with an almost perfect extra-cover drive, Vaughan has often appeared on the verge of greatness but has only occasionally attained it. Across three consecutive series in 2002 – against Sri Lanka, India and Australia – he hit seven centuries in 12 innings at a combined average of 69.68. This purple patch took to him No1 in the world batting rankings, but he was never again able to sustain such a run, and his record is tarnished by several unnecessary dismissals.

But Vaughan's career was protected against these blips by his innovative captaincy. He skippered England in 51 Tests (second only to Michael Atherton) and his 26 Test victories are more than any other England captain. He took his place in the history books in 2005 when he led his team to a brilliant Ashes victory. Another personal highlight was the 2007 Headingley Test against the Windies when, after a year out with injury, he hit a gutsy 104. In 2007 he lost the one-day captaincy, and in August 2008 resigned as Test captain.

2

A batsman hits the ball straight down the pitch. His partner turns his back on the ball but it becomes caught in his loosely strapped pad. The batsman shakes the ball loose and as it rolls away they run a quick single. The fielding captain insists it doesn't count. What is your decision?

TREVILLION

3

A bowler finishes his over just before both teams leave the field because of a heavy rain shower. Three hours later, when you resume play, the bowler who finished the over before the rain interruption now wants to bowl the first over from the other end. The fielding captain insists a bowler cannot bowl two consecutive overs. What is your decision?

Answers

1) If a batsman leaves the wicket thinking he's out but you would have given him not out, the umpire can intervene and call him back.

2) The run doesn't count. If the ball lodges in the clothing or equipment of either batsmen, or the umpires, it becomes dead. No runs can be scored or wickets taken.

1

A batsman goes down the pitch to a slow bowler, but misses the ball, which turns so sharply it ends up in the first slip's hands. He steps forward and breaks the wicket. The non-striker hasn't left his crease seeing the inevitable run-out if he attempts to run. Do you give the batsman out stumped, or run out? Why?

TREVILLION.

Merv Hughes

Full name: Mervyn Gregory Hughes
Date of birth: November 23, 1961
Major teams: Australia, Victoria, Essex

Tests: **53**	ODIs: **33**
Ave: **16.64**	Ave: **11.11**
Fifties: **2**	Wickets: **38**
Wickets: **212**	Bowling ave: **29.34**
Bowling ave: **28.38**	BBM: **4-44**
BBI: **8-87**	
BBM: **13-217**	

Merv is a true Aussie cult hero, thanks to his trademark moustache, his sense of humour and almost legendary consumption of food and alcohol. But underneath all that was a dedicated and effective fast bowler. After a not especially glorious early international career he took a complicated hat-trick – achieved over three different days – and combined figures of 13 for 217 in the second Test against West Indies in 1988-89.

His bowling began to improve as he matured, with added control and a more judicious use of his bouncer. He also proved to be an agricultural yet useful lower-order batsman. These attributes helped him to reach his career highpoint: spearheading Australia's 4-1 Ashes defeat of England in 1993 by taking 31 wickets. However, a knee injury sustained during that series kept him out for over half a year and, after just two more Tests, he was forced to retire. He remains involved in Australian cricket and became a national selector in 2005.

2 A fielder leaves his cap outside the boundary rope. A spectator sees the ball racing away for a boundary, so picks up the cap and throws it at the ball in an attempt to stop it. The cap does hit the ball, but the ball carries on to the boundary. Do you give the four or award five penalty runs?

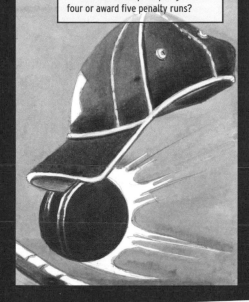

3 You've dispensed with the bails due to windy conditions. Next ball, the batsman swipes and misses, but the ball only trickles into the stumps. The batsman stands his ground saying that, had the bails still been on, the ball wouldn't have disturbed them. What is your decision?

Answers

1) Give the batsman run out on appeal. The law is clear: only a wicketkeeper can stump a batsman. In this instance the ball went to the slip fielder who broke the wicket, so the batsman is run out rather than stumped.

2) Award four runs for the boundary. Only a member of the fielding side can be guilty of illegal fielding, not a spectator. If a fielder had used his cap illegally you would award the penalty runs.

3) Out, bowled, on appeal. When bails are dispensed with, the ball only has to strike the stumps. In this instance the law doesn't say how hard the wicket has to be struck for the batsman to be given out, merely that it does so.

1 A fielder takes a catch just inside the boundary rope. In celebration he throws the ball into the air but, instead of coming straight back down, the ball goes over his head and over the boundary. The fielder claims the catch but the batsman insists it's a four – because the fielder did not have hold of the ball long enough. What is your decision?

2 A batsman offers no shot to a delivery that flicks the pad. The non-striker calls for a single but, in his haste, doesn't ground his bat properly, creating a short run. They attempt a second run but the batsman fails to make his ground at the wicketkeeper's end as the bails are removed. The fielding side appeal. What do you give?

KEY MOMENT

Shaun Pollock

Australia v South Africa
Adelaide, 30 Jan to 3 Feb 1998
First innings: 7-87
Second innings: 2-61
Match drawn

Shaun Pollock returned his best Test innings figures against Australia, when he took seven for 87 from their first innings. With the bat he had scored 40 to help South Africa to a first innings total of 517. With the ball, though, he tore through a great Australia side, including the key scalps of both Waugh brothers. Australia were limited to 350 – a deficit of 167 – and Pollock had made it all but impossible for his opponents to win the match. In their second innings he was less effective, taking two wickets for 61 runs, and Australia eventually batted out a draw, principally due to a battling 115 from Mark Waugh.
Full biography, page 79

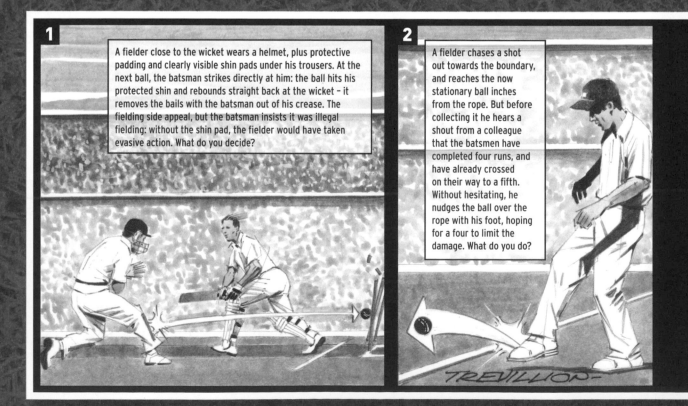

1 A fielder close to the wicket wears a helmet, plus protective padding and clearly visible shin pads under his trousers. At the next ball, the batsman strikes directly at him: the ball hits his protected shin and rebounds straight back at the wicket – it removes the bails with the batsman out of his crease. The fielding side appeal, but the batsman insists it was illegal fielding: without the shin pad, the fielder would have taken evasive action. What do you decide?

2 A fielder chases a shot out towards the boundary, and reaches the now stationary ball inches from the rope. But before collecting it he hears a shout from a colleague that the batsmen have completed four runs, and have already crossed on their way to a fifth. Without hesitating, he nudges the ball over the rope with his foot, hoping for a four to limit the damage. What do you do?

3

An artificial pitch has a one inch wide rim of wood all around the outside of the wicket, almost flush with the ground. The bowler bowls a very wide ball to a right-handed batsman but it hits the inside of the rim, turns right and bowls him. Your colleague calls 'dead ball' and gives him out. The fielding captain asks for an explanation and your colleague says he'll call and signal dead ball every time the ball hits the rim, regardless of the outcome. Is he right?

Answers

1) If, in your view, the fielder had control of the ball, give the batsman out. If not, award four runs. You must be certain whether the catcher has control of the ball and of his further movement and make your decision based on this. The umpires alone must decide on the fairness of the catch: it's normally the bowler's end umpire's decision but he can consult his colleague if necessary.

2) Not out. If the batsman offers no shot to a delivery then no runs can be scored. The batsmen are allowed to run one run only to allow the fielding side the chance of a run-out. As soon as that run is completed the bowler's end umpire would call and signal 'dead ball' – not allowing the wicket to be taken. No run would be scored and the ball would count in that over.

3) No, it's not the correct decision. Umpires have to perform certain pre-match duties. At the toss you and your colleague should have clearly informed both captains that they'd call dead ball if the ball struck the wooden rim. They cannot make up regulations once play has begun and so cannot rule on the dismissal – so the batsman is not out. Equally, if you'd pre-arranged that the ball would be called dead when it hit the wooden rim, no further developments can ensue once it has been called dead.

Stuart Broad

Full name: Stuart Christopher John Broad
Date of birth: June 24, 1986
Major teams: England, Leicestershire, Nottinghamshire

Tests: 9	ODIs: 42
Ave: 37.20	Ave: 20.28
Fifties: 3	High score: 45*
High score: 76	Wickets: 62
Wickets: 24	Bowling ave: 27.58
Bowling ave: 43.41	BBM: 5-23
BBI: 3-44 BBM: 5-104	

Stuart Broad, son of former England opener Chris, broke into the England squad at the end of 2007 against Sri Lanka. Though his debut was unremarkable, at the age of just 21 he had such evident talent that it was obvious he was a player worth persevering with. Initially, he had wished to be a batsman, but a sudden growth spurt in his teens led him to take up pace bowling. Within a few years he was playing for England. But despite being picked for his bowling, it was his batting that impressed: he scored three fifties in his first nine Tests and proved himself to be the answer to England's problematic No8 position. A back-foot drive on his toes received particular praise.

However, while his batting surpassed expectations, his bowling has often been unexceptional. Although rarely wayward and generally economical, he failed to take wickets at a high enough rate, and suffered the humiliation of being hit for six sixes in one over in the Twenty20 World Cup by India's Yuvraj Singh in 2007. Nevertheless, with the fundamentals of his bowling technique secure – height, bounce and intelligence – and his composure with the bat evident, Broad has the potential to mature into a genuine all-rounder.

3

A captain declares in fading light in order to give his two exceptionally fast bowlers time to get in at least four overs. But the opposition captain reacts by sending in two tailenders. He's hoping that you'll decide that the fading light, although still playable for specialist opening batsmen, is too dangerous for the two weaker batsmen. How do you react?

Answers

1) Run out on appeal. This wasn't illegal fielding. The law on protective equipment refers only to external equipment, and as the shin pads are under the fielder's trousers, even though clearly visible, they are not illegal. Only the wicketkeeper is allowed to wear external pads.

2) Award nine runs: the four completed, another one because the batsmen have crossed, and a four-run penalty for the fielder kicking the ball over the boundary. John Holder: Ian Blackwell of Somerset did this in a county match at Northampton. After a long chase to the boundary he kicked the ball over the rope to prevent the batsmen from running five. The completed runs were awarded, plus a five-run penalty, which was incorrect. It should have been a four-run penalty.

3) The fading light must be suitable for any batsman, whether specialist or tailender. The batting captain, aware that the opposition has two very fast bowlers armed with a new ball, has the responsibility to ensure that the batsmen he selects can cope. As long as, in your opinion, the bowling is neither dangerous or unfair, play would proceed.

1

A batsman complains that the wicketkeeper is standing too close, and leaning over the wicket until the bowler's final delivery stride. He says it restricts him from playing a round-house pull shot. He insists the wicketkeeper must stand a bat's length from the stumps. What is your decision?

2

A fast bowler, who delivers the ball close to the wicket, asks that you move to the side and take three steps back, saying that your position directly behind the stumps is both a hindrance and a distraction. How do you react?

Dennis Lillee

Full name: Dennis Keith Lillee
Date of birth: July 18, 1949
Major teams: Australia, Tasmania, Northamptonshire, Western Australia

Tests: 70
Ave: 13.71
Fifties: 1
High score: 73*
Wickets: 355
Bowling ave: 23.92
BBI: 7-83 **BBM:** 11-123

ODIs: 63
Ave: 9.23
Wickets: 103
Bowling ave: 20.82
BBM: 5-34

One of the most talented, and most terrifying, fast bowlers ever, Dennis Lillee ended his career with a then-record 355 Test wickets. Until an injury suffered on tour to Pakistan in 1972-73, Lillee took these wickets with devastating pace. The injury, a stress fracture, threatened his career and, though he recovered through physiotherapy, it kept him out of the game for three years. When he returned it was with a remodelled action. He'd lost some of his blistering pace but had gained accuracy and a purity of technique.

Many of Lillee's wickets were taken in tandem with fellow fast bowling legend Jeff Thomson, and together they terrorised batsmen, particularly English ones. His other key partner was wicketkeeper Rodney Marsh, with whom he combined to take a world-record 95 Test victims. With 23 five-wicket hauls his highlights were many, but his best match figures – 11/123 – were achieved against England while his 10 wickets against West Indies in 1981 also helped deliver an important win.

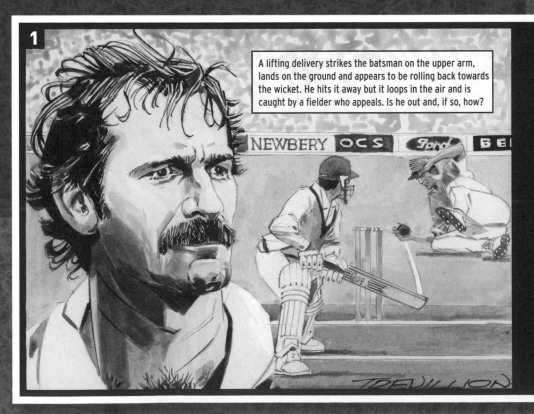

1

A lifting delivery strikes the batsman on the upper arm, lands on the ground and appears to be rolling back towards the wicket. He hits it away but it loops in the air and is caught by a fielder who appeals. Is he out and, if so, how?

3

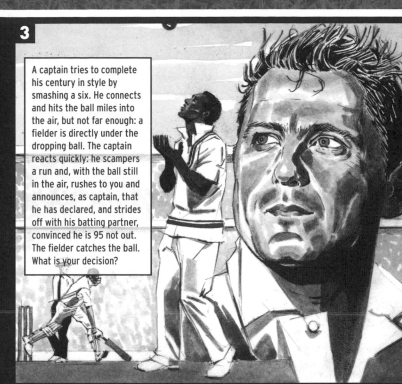

A captain tries to complete his century in style by smashing a six. He connects and hits the ball miles into the air, but not far enough: a fielder is directly under the dropping ball. The captain reacts quickly: he scampers a run and, with the ball still in the air, rushes to you and announces, as captain, that he has declared, and strides off with his batting partner, convinced he is 95 not out. The fielder catches the ball. What is your decision?

Answers

1) Dismiss his complaint. The striker cannot insist the keeper stands back to allow him to play a round-house shot: it's up to the wicketkeeper to take evasive action. If, however, at the moment of delivery, any part of the wicketkeeper's equipment or person is in front of the wicket, signal no ball.

2) Dismiss his complaint. The bowler cannot dictate where you stand. You need to be directly behind the wicket to judge lbws, and close to it to check the position of the bowler's front foot. John Holder: During a county match at Hove several years ago I was asked to move back by Adrian Jones of Sussex, a fast bowler who had bowled several no balls. I refused, telling him I would only move back if he delivered from further behind the popping crease. He wasn't best pleased.

3) Out on appeal. The law has been rewritten to prevent this blatant gamesmanship, one of WG Grace's favourite tricks. Not until the catch is completed does the ball become dead – only then can he declare.

Darren Gough

Full name: Darren Gough
Date of birth: September 18, 1970
Major teams: England, Yorkshire, Essex

Tests: 58
Ave: 12.57
Fifties: 2
Wickets: 229
Bowling ave: 28.39
BBI: 6-42 BBM: 9-92

ODIs: 159
Ave: 12.42
Wickets: 235
Bowling ave: 26.42
BBM: 5-44

Darren Gough was England's leading fast bowler of the 1990s. Injuries and a tendency towards self-aggrandisement meant he was often underappreciated, but Gough was a world-class fast bowler. Shorter than a standard modern pace bowler – and, therefore, without a real bouncer – he had to develop and create more inventive means of taking his wickets, mastering reverse swing and possessing a devilish yorker. This brought him success in Test cricket, where he sits ninth on England's wicket-takers list, with 229 scalps. But it was in ODIs that his tricks really thrived: he has, by a considerable distance, taken more wickets in one-dayers than any other England player.

Exuberant and extrovert, 'Dazzler' struggled with injuries throughout his career, and a knee injury against New Zealand in 2002 curtailed his Test involvement. He managed, largely through his ability to talk himself into selection, to prolong his ODI career, where his experience and cunning allowed him to remain effective. He enjoyed an equally fruitful county career but, after captaining Yorkshire between 2006 and 2008, he announced his retirement from all forms of cricket. He's now a TV personality.

2

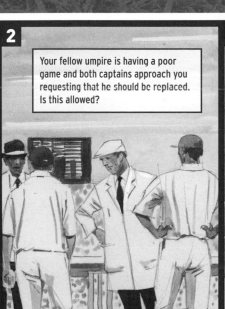

Your fellow umpire is having a poor game and both captains approach you requesting that he should be replaced. Is this allowed?

3

A fielder is injured and is replaced by the twelfth man. Soon afterwards the wicketkeeper pulls a muscle and has to leave the field. His captain wants the twelfth man to keep wicket, but both batsmen object. Do you allow him to keep wicket?

Answers

1) Not out. The striker is allowed to hit the ball twice or more in defence of his wicket, but he can only be given out caught from the first strike, or if the ball hasn't touched the ground before he hits it again.

2) No. An umpire can only be changed during a match due to exceptional circumstances, such as illness or injury. If there is a change, the replacement can only officiate from square leg, unless both captains agree for him to take full umpiring responsibilities. John Holder: In a one-day match between Somerset and Notts, my colleague David Shepherd went to move out of the way as the batsmen went for a quick run. He suddenly pulled up clutching his left calf. I called dead ball and he was helped off the field. As there was no other first-class umpire present, I officiated at both ends and the former Somerset spinner Peter Robinson did the square leg duties. Soon after he gave Notts' Darren Bicknell out, run out. Although the batsman was unhappy, the TV replay vindicated Peter.

3) No. A substitute can field in any position except wicketkeeper. That position must be taken by one of the 11 nominated players, except under a special regulation that allows it, with the permission of the opposing captain.

1 A bowler races in behind you to deliver but, as he does so, clips the wicket at your end with his boot. The bail falls, the bowler's rhythm is upset and he drops the ball, which bounces slowly up the pitch to the batsman. The batsman takes aim and hits it crisply away and completes a run. What is your decision?

2 The first day of a Test match is lost to rain. The side batting first make 450 by lunch on day three, then bowl their opponents out for 280. The side with the lead want to enforce the follow-on as the match has become a four-day game and they lead by more than 150 runs. Their opponents insist the follow-on mark is still 200. Who is correct?

Answers

1) If, as in this case, the ball bounces more than twice but does not come to a stop before reaching the striker, you will call 'no ball', but the run will be credited to the striker and the no ball penalty to extras. Had the ball not reached the striker, you would call 'no ball', followed by 'dead ball', and the batsman has no right to hit the ball. John Holder: In the late eighties, at a County Championship match between Nottinghamshire and Northamptonshire, I was umpiring at point when Curtly Ambrose lost control of the ball during his delivery. It looped high in the air and dropped at forward short leg, in front of batsman Derek Randall. His eyes lit up as he saw the chance of some easy runs: he teed up the ball and smacked it to midwicket for four. Turning round he saw Ambrose (a good foot taller) towering over him with a face like thunder. Realising he would have to face a pumped-up Ambrose and his ability to deliver fearsome beamers, Randall looked to bowler's end umpire Merv Kitchen and shouted: 'Merv, I don't want those runs – cancel them!' Of course Merv couldn't cancel the runs but everyone fell about laughing and Curtly, ever the professional, let Derek off with just one of his normal, blisteringly fast deliveries with the next ball.

2) Because it has become a four-day match the follow-on total is indeed 150 runs not 200. So they can enforce the follow-on.

3) Attempting to steal a run during a bowler's run-up is not allowed. The four runs will not count. You will call 'dead ball', return the batsmen to their original ends, award five penalty runs to the fielding side and both batsmen will be reported to the authorities.

3 As the bowler starts a very long run-up to deliver, the batsmen decide to quickly steal a run as he approaches the wicket. The 'non-facing' batsman then hammers the delivery for four. What is your decision?

Donald Bradman

Full name: Sir Donald George Bradman
Date of birth: August 27, 1908
Major teams: Australia, New South Wales, South Australia

Tests: 52
Ave: 99.94
Centuries: 29
Fifties: 13
High score: 334

Don Bradman was, without doubt, the greatest batsman to have ever played the game. No cricketer has approached his standard and, arguably, no other sportsman has matched his complete dominance. A Test average of over 50 is considered a mark of greatness – but Bradman's final figure was 99.94. He holds many Test records to this day, including the highest ratio of centuries per innings (29 from 80), the most double centuries (12), and the most consecutive matches in which he made centuries (six).

Bradman's success was founded upon a simple yet unorthodox technique. Keeping his head straight, his bat initially stationed between his legs, he would draw up his blade with a crooked backswing – the result of a unique grip. This allowed him to keep the ball down: he very rarely lifted it. His small stature meant that he favoured a horizontal bat and scored many runs through hooks and pulls. He wasn't elegant, but, when combined with rare powers of concentration and discipline, his technique ensured that he was perhaps the hardest ever batsman to dislodge.

As a captain, in 1948, he led Australia on an undefeated tour of England – the first time a Test side had toured without a single loss – an achievement that earned them the nickname The Invincibles. He died in 2001.

Colin Cowdrey

Full name:
Michael Colin Cowdrey
Date of birth:
December 24, 1932
Major teams:
England, Kent

Tests: 114
Ave: 44.06
Centuries: 22
Fifties: 38
High Score: 182

With a first-class cricketer for a father and MCC as his initials, Colin Cowdrey seemed destined to become a cricketer. And, sure enough, as a young man he was a prodigy: taking eight wickets and scoring 75 as a 13-year-old at Lord's, scoring 90 for Kent aged just 18 and, when only 21, being capped for England and scoring a 100 in his third Test. Ostensibly, he used this natural talent to the full – he was the first Englishman to play in 100 Tests and, with 22 centuries, is joint record-holder for the most centuries for his country. This success was founded on an immaculate technique, a steadfast defence and a cover-drive that was often compared to Wally Hammond's.

However, there were mumbles of a psychological flaw: an indecisiveness, a lack of aggression. He shined principally against top teams and occasionally appeared to lack the fight for county cricket and against second-rate Test sides. That perception was perhaps the reason that, though he captained England in 27 Tests, he was only ever handed the role as a stand-in or a second-choice. He was not, it was agreed, a natural leader. Nevertheless he was a fabulously talented cricketer and, in later years, a fine sporting ambassador. In 1997 he became only the second cricketer to be elevated to the House of Lord's. He died in 2000.

1 A wicketkeeper, suffering from hay fever, sneezes very loudly just as the bowler releases his delivery, distracting the batsman, who is bowled. What is your decision?

1 A legal delivery passing close to the bat strikes the batsman on the pad in front of the stumps, loops up and is caught. Both the fielder and the bowler appeal for a bat-pad catch. You're not absolutely sure if the ball touched the bat – but you are confident that the batsman was out lbw. What do you decide?

2 A batsman shoulders arms to a ball as it passes through to the wicketkeeper. The batsman holds the pose then brings his bat back down – but clips a bail, which falls off. The ball is still in the keeper's gloves. Is he out on appeal?

Answers

1) The 'How's that?' appeal covers every form of dismissal: bowled, stumped, run out etc. Once an appeal is made, it's up to you, not the players, whether a batsman is out, and now he's out. So in this instance, the batsman is out lbw, and you should signal this to the scorers for clarification.

2) You have to consider if the ball is dead. In my opinion: it's dead. John Holder: after the ball went through to the wicketkeeper, enough time had elapsed for it to be safely assumed that the ball was dead, and that neither team was looking for any further action. There's no specific time frame for this – it's up to your judgment. In this case I'd say the ball was dead in the keeper's gloves, so the batsman was not out.

3) At the moment of delivery there can be only two fielders behind square on the leg side – but that doesn't include the wicketkeeper. So no, this is not a no ball.

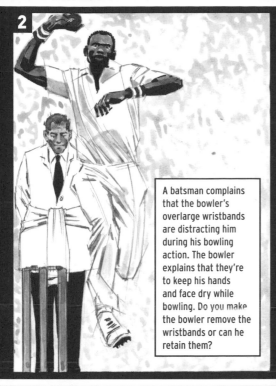

2 A batsman complains that the bowler's overlarge wristbands are distracting him during his bowling action. The bowler explains that they're to keep his hands and face dry while bowling. Do you make the bowler remove the wristbands or can he retain them?

3 A batsman plays a defensive stroke and the ball bounces at his feet, spins backwards and nudges his off stump. He turns quickly and stops the bail from being dislodged by pressing down on it with his bat. What is your decision?

Answers

1) Not out. You should react quickly: either umpire can immediately call, and signal, dead ball, because the striker was clearly distracted by the keeper sneezing, which caused him to be bowled. The ball would not count in that over.

2) The batsman's complaint is a fair one: you should make the bowler remove the wristband on his bowling arm because it's clearly causing a distraction.

3) Quite a clever attempt on his part, but it's still out. If the batsman prevents the ball from being dislodged off a legitimate delivery, it is obstruction and he is given out on appeal.

Graham Gooch

Full name: Graham Alan Gooch
Date of birth: July 23, 1953
Major teams: England, Essex, Western Province

Tests: 118	ODIs: 125
Ave: 42.58	Ave: 36.98
Centuries: 20	Centuries: 8
Fifties: 46	Fifties: 23
High score: 333	High score: 142
Wickets: 23	Wickets: 36

Despite scoring a pair on his debut against Australia, Graham Gooch went on to have a record-breaking, 20-year Test career. His personal zenith was the Lord's Test against India in 1990 when he scored 333 in the first innings (the highest score by an England player since 1938) and 123 in the second – an aggregate score of 456, and a world record of runs scored in a Test.

Gooch started as a walloper, but his style evolved as he matured. And his character was more complicated than his countenance suggested: he caused much controversy by leading a rebel tour to South Africa in 1982 – an act for which he was banned from Test cricket for three years. He was appointed captain in 1988 and, though his reign didn't endear him to all, he imposed the discipline that the side required. Gooch's spectacular longevity allowed him to score the most Test runs for England and, if you take into consideration List A one-day matches as well, he scored 67,057 top-level runs, more than any other player. He was also a stalwart for Essex, scoring 94 centuries and 30,701 runs, both records.

3 A left-arm fast bowler bowls round the wicket to a right-handed batsman. The wicketkeeper moves to the leg side of the stumps – near a fine leg and backward square leg. There are now three fielders behind square on the leg side. Is it a no ball?

1 A substitute fielder is on the pitch when a wicket falls. Several balls after play restarts you notice that the twelfth man has left and the original player is back on and has just fielded the ball. What action do you take?

2 It's the height of summer, temperatures are soaring and the grass is dying in parts of the square. At the close of play that evening the groundsmen ask for permission to water the pitch that evening to keep the grass alive. Do you allow them to do so?

TREVILLION

Answers

1) Award five penalty runs to the batting side. A fielder must always ask your permission to return to the field. If he doesn't, and then fields the ball while it is live, the ball doesn't count in the over and you must award penalty runs. In 2001 this happened in a county match at Northampton. Ian Blackwell of Somerset, having batted and scored a century, didn't come out to field when Northampton began their innings. Unknown to the umpires the twelfth man was on as a substitute; he fielded the ball so five penalty runs were awarded to the batting side.

2) No. The pitch cannot be watered. Once the toss has been made it's the sole responsibility of the umpires and they would not allow it to be watered mid-match.

3) Yes, at any time during the match both captains may agree to forego the tea interval, but the umpires must be notified.

HUTTON AND ENGLAND SMASH RECORDS

Injury to Bradman a Crushing Blow; Brown Stands Alone in the Last Ditch

A MATCH TAKEN OUT OF THE REALM OF CRICKET

By Neville Cardus (Cricketer)

ENGLAND.—First Innings.

Hutton c Hassett b O'Reilly	364
Edrich lbw b O'Reilly	12
Leyland run out	187
W. R. Hammond lbw b F'twood-Smith	59
Paynter lbw b O'Reilly	0
Compton b Waite	1
Hardstaff not out	169
Wood c and b Barnes	53
Verity not out	8
B 22, lb 19, w 1, nb 8	50

Total (for seven wickets) 903
Innings declared.

K. Farnes and Bowes did not bat.

BOWLING ANALYSIS.
ENGLAND.—First Innings.

	O.	M.	R.	W.
Waite	72	16	150	1
McCabe	38	8	85	0
O'Reilly	85	26	178	3
Fleetwood-Smith	87	11	298	1
Barnes	38	3	84	1
Hassett	13	2	52	0
Bradman	3	2	6	0

Waite bowled one wide, O'Reilly seven no-balls, and Fleetwood-Smith one no-ball.

Fall of the Wickets:

1	2	3	4	5	6	7
29	411	516	547	555	770	876

AUSTRALIA.—First Innings.

C. L. Badcock c Hardstaff b Bowes	0
W. A. Brown not out	48
S. J. McCabe c Edrich b Farnes	29
A. L. Hassett c Compton b Edrich	14
S. Barnes not out	41
B 4, lb 2, nb 1	25

Total (for three wickets) 117

To bat: D. G. Bradman, B. A. Barnett, J. H. Fingleton, M. G. Waite, W. J. O'Reilly, and L. O'B. Fleetwood-Smith.

BOWLING ANALYSIS TO DATE
AUSTRALIA.—First Innings.

	O.	M.	R.	W.
Farnes	9	2	42	1
Bowes	9	2	21	1
Edrich	5	0	21	1
Verity	5	1	15	0
Leyland	2	0	5	0

Fall of the Wickets:

1	2	3
0	19	70

Umpires: Chester and Walden.

THE OVAL, TUESDAY.

This afternoon just before tea Bradman was bowling and England were 887 for seven, which was the equal of the highest score ever made in a first-class match in England. Suddenly Bradman fell to the ground in utter collapse...

only all over this country. People walking down Collins Street in Melbourne would hear it, and it would roar and echo in Kandy, Calcutta, Allahabad, Penang; they would hear it in the Cocos Islands and join in, and on liners going patiently their ways over the seven seas they would hear it too, and drink Hutton's health. Possibly in some club in Pall Mall a permanent member would wake up and go to the lunch-room and have to be informed who was Hutton.

England proceeded to beat the Australian record of the highest total amassed in a Test match. Little effort was made to increase the rate of scoring. Loose stuff was pushed for careful ones or twos whether McCabe was swinging his arm or any more authentic bowler. At lunch the score was 758 for five, and I observed now a number of Chelsea veterans watching the cricket. I wondered how many of them would live to see the match finished.

Out at Last

After lunch Hardstaff reached his hundred, then at half-past two Hutton got out through sheer exhaustion, caught at cover. His extraordinary innings lasted some thirteen hours and a quarter and he gave an easy chance of stumping when he was 40. He and Hardstaff added 215 for the sixth wicket in three and a half hours; I apologise for these statistics, but there was nothing else to write about. A new game has been invented which employs the implements of cricket.

At 770 for six another Yorkshireman came forth, rugged and ready to hold the fort. But Wood at once hit a boundary or two; the habits of a lifetime are hard to forget. The

win with the last men batting. Bradman's fielding and his eager and sensible captaincy throughout a fearful ordeal were beyond praise; he nursed his bowlers, talked to them, put his arm in theirs between overs, and cheered them up; he was not only the team's captain but the father-confessor and philosopher.

A Wrong Spirit

Hardstaff persisted in stone-walling, probably under orders. Such is contemporary Test cricket in this our England. Wood compiled 50 in 65 minutes, but in spite of his lack of conscience in the cause England scored only 100 runs in 100 minutes between lunch and four o'clock, against an attack which frequently consisted of Hassett and Barnes. Apologists blamed the played-out Test match for this state of things, but what was wrong was the spirit of the batting. If the spirit is wrong, the game will be wrong under any conditions. Hardstaff increased his score by 48 in an hour and three-quarters after passing his hundred and England more than 750 in hand for six. Wood was caught and bowled at 876, the seventh out, and when he reluctantly departed, with eight fours much to his credit, Hardstaff had acquired 150 in nearly five hours. And, by the way, when Wood got out Yorkshire in the match had scored 604 for three wickets.

At a quarter-past four the day's tragedy occurred. Bradman was carried off the field. Shortly afterwards Hammond mercifully declared England's innings closed at 903 for seven, no doubt to the great relief of the men who work the scoreboards, for there is no room on them for a total of four figures.

At five o'clock, in a mellow light, the Australians began their forlorn journey and ran into hardship straightway, for in Bowes's first over Badcock lamely pushed a ball into the hands of close mid-on, a stroke of little or no conviction. The scoreboard now read 0—1—0, a curious sight, like a once prosperous firm gone bankrupt, carpets taken up, and nothing left but vacancy. McCabe got a single from Farnes and a fortuitous four through the slips, and Farnes beat him again. The men...

3 In a tense match both captains are anxious for a result as a draw is no good to either side. There's rain in the air and more is due later, so both sides want to forego the tea interval and continue playing. Do you allow them to do so?

Len Hutton

Full name: Sir Leonard Hutton
Date of birth: June 23, 1916
Major teams: England, Yorkshire

Tests: 79
Ave: 56.67
Centuries: 19
Fifties: 33
High score: 364

If Denis Compton provided the glamour and style for English cricket after the war, Sir Leonard Hutton provided attributes just as vital: discipline and reliability. He made his debut, pre-war, for Yorkshire aged just 17, and, at 20, played for England, for whom he hit a century in his second Test. After the war, though, he became a much more conservative batsman, trading the flair he certainly possessed for patient accumulation.

Such was his worth to the England side that, in 1952, he was appointed the country's first professional captain for 65 years – a position that, remarkably, he was never offered at Yorkshire. As captain and dominant batsman he took England to some notable successes, including a 3-1 Ashes victory in 1954-55.

His personal highlight was a monumental 364 against Australia in 1938; it was a then-world record and remains the highest Test score by an Englishman. In all he scored 19 centuries and 6,971 Test runs at an average of 56.67; in first-class cricket he scored over 40,000 runs and hit 129 centuries. Quite simply, Hutton, who died in 1990, will be remembered as one of England's greatest ever batsmen.

KEY MOMENT

Alastair Cook

India v England
Nagpur, 1-5 March 2006
First innings: 60 runs,
206 mins, 160 balls, 7 fours.
Second innings: 104*, 364
mins, 243 balls, 12 fours.
Match drawn

Not much was expected of Alastair Cook on his debut. Aged just 21 he was picked because of Michael Vaughan's injury and the last-minute withdrawal of Marcus Trescothick. When he was summoned he was on an England 'A' tour of the West Indies, so had to travel halfway around the globe to reach Nagpur. In his first international innings he was bowled by all-rounder Irfan Pathan for 60. Cook later developed a puzzling tendency to be dismissed in the 60s – doing so 10 times in his first 34 Tests – but at the time it was an impressive start. He batted with real composure and maturity and displayed a technique more than capable of coping with the demands of Test cricket.

In his second innings he formed partnerships with Andrew Strauss and Paul Collingwood on his way to his debut century, becoming the 16th Englishman to score a ton in his first Test match. England declared on 297, having waited for Cook to pass his milestone for an unbeaten 104, in an ultimately futile attempt to force a result. Though India batted out a draw, Cook had excelled and was immediately hailed as a future great.

Full biography, page 80.

1 A bowler is constantly following through down the middle of the pitch after his deliveries, despite your warnings. Can he be sent off the field for persistently disobeying you?

TREVILLION

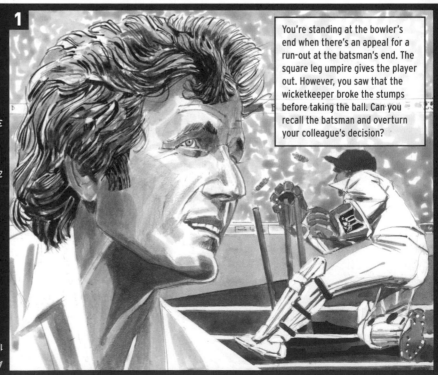

1 You're standing at the bowler's end when there's an appeal for a run-out at the batsman's end. The square leg umpire gives the player out. However, you saw that the wicketkeeper broke the stumps before taking the ball. Can you recall the batsman and overturn your colleague's decision?

Answers

1) No, you can't overturn his decision. It's up to him. Because good umpires work together, you would instead call 'dead ball', tell the batsman to wait, then consult your colleague, telling him what you saw. John Holder: Several years ago in a one-day match at Lord's, my colleague was standing at the bowler's end. The ball was driven hard to mid-off and he raced to the off side to get in line with the popping crease, shielding his head in case the ball was thrown towards the keeper. The fielder threw the ball at the bowler's wicket, shattering it with the striker short of his ground. As my colleague didn't see what happened behind his back, he had to give it not out, and refused to reverse his decision.

2) b) Out caught on appeal. The ball didn't touch the boundary rope or fence or the ground beyond it. And no part of the fielder's person was in contact with, or grounded over, the fence or rope.

3) No. Cancel all runs scored and return both batsmen to their original ends. The state of the game and the distance by which he is short of his ground will tell you if the running short was deliberate. If there's any repeat by any member of the team in that innings, repeat the process above and award five penalty runs to the fielding side. A report will also be sent to the governing body.

2 A wicket falls to the last ball before lunch and the players leave the field. After the break, the not-out batsman returns with a new partner, but, before you can call 'play', it begins to rain and the players leave the field again. When play resumes the not-out batsman returns with a different partner. Do you allow it?

3

The ball hits the striker's pad, rebounds on to his bat, then hits his wicket and a bail falls. On appeal, the other umpire gives him out lbw, on the basis that this was the first occurrence. Is he correct?

Answers

1) No. Only a captain can send one of his players off the field: you have no authority to do this. The procedure is this: warn the bowler after the first infringement, informing his captain, both batsmen and the other umpire. If there's a further breach a second and final warning will be issued, informing the same people. If he infringes again, the captain will be instructed to take the bowler off, and he cannot bowl for the rest of the innings. John Holder: In practice the bowler will also receive an initial, friendly warning, pointing out what he is doing wrong and advising him to avoid the protected area. I've had to ban a bowler for running on the pitch only twice and both times it was Stuart Lampitt, the former Worcestershire seam bowler. He liked to get as close to the wicket as possible while bowling but would invariably follow through on to the protected area.

2) Yes. As 'play' had not been called, the innings of the previous partner had not actually begun – so the batting side can choose a different new batsman.

3) No. The correct decision would have been out, bowled. Whenever there are two competing methods of dismissal, and one of them is bowled, it always takes precedence.

Bob Willis

Full name: Robert George Dylan Willis
Date of birth: May 30, 1949
Major teams: England, Surrey, Warwickshire, Northern Transvaal

Tests: 90	ODIs: 64
Ave: 11.50	Ave: 10.37
Wickets: 325	Wickets: 80
Bowling ave: 25.20	Bowling ave: 24.60
BBI: 8-43 BBM: 9-92	BBM: 4-11

England have rarely had a faster bowler than Bob Willis. He largely avoided swing and seam, instead relying on a 30-yard run-up and a peculiar gangling gait to generate genuine pace. Though he enjoyed a hugely successful career, he was hindered by a series of injuries. Knee surgery in 1975 ensured that he was never quite free from pain for the rest of his career. He did, however, keep running in for a further 10 years.

Despite taking 325 Test wickets, Willis is largely remembered for his role in the 1981 Headingley Test against Australia. Together with Ian Botham, Willis rescued England from an apparently certain defeat, recording a haul of 8/43 in the second innings. He also captained England in 18 Tests, more than any other bowler.

---

2 A ball hit by the batsman is heading over the boundary rope for a six. The ball crosses the line but is still in the air when a fielder leaps and palms the ball back over the rope, then takes a remarkable catch. His feet were in the air when he made contact with the ball. Is it a) a six, b) out, or c) a dead ball?

3 A side with nine wickets down and ten runs to win has a star batsman in good form, batting with the world's worst number 11. In trying to run a two to keep the strike the good batsman runs 'one short'. Does he stay on strike and get a single?

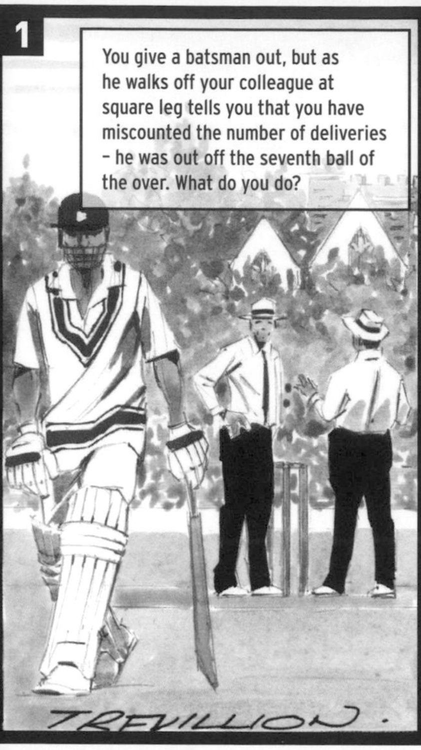
1
You give a batsman out, but as he walks off your colleague at square leg tells you that you have miscounted the number of deliveries – he was out off the seventh ball of the over. What do you do?
TREVILLION.

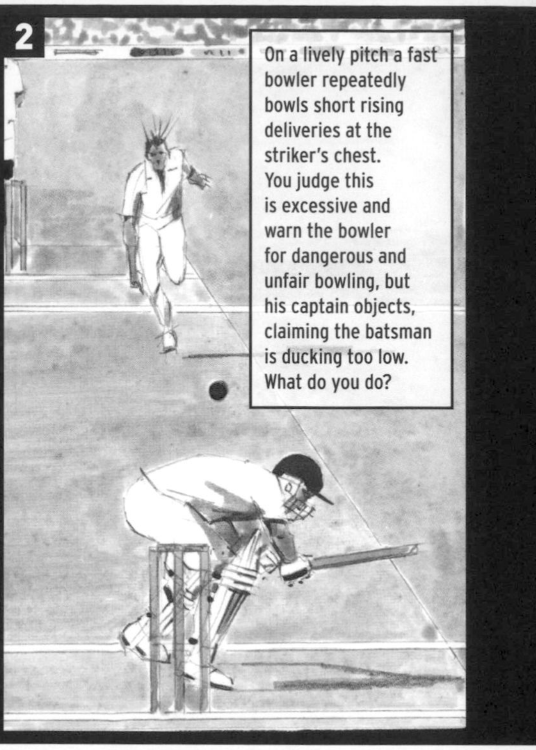
2
On a lively pitch a fast bowler repeatedly bowls short rising deliveries at the striker's chest. You judge this is excessive and warn the bowler for dangerous and unfair bowling, but his captain objects, claiming the batsman is ducking too low. What do you do?

6ft 4in, followed through and stood towering over Langer (5ft 6in) glaring at him. Langer defiantly glared back. The battle hotted up as Langer drove, pulled, cut and hooked Donald to all parts, racing to 50 from 25 deliveries. But, despite the aggressive body language of both combatants, no words were exchanged between them. However, I could hear Donald muttering 'That little Aussie b******' to himself as he walked past me to his mark. Langer raced to 70 and Donald was replaced by Dougie Brown at my end. He bowled a wide half volley first ball and Langer, trying to hit it square on the off side, dragged it onto his wicket. As he left the wicket, walking from the Nursery End past Donald at extra cover, Donald said: 'Well played.' An excellent example of true sportsmanship. Langer had received a fair share of vicious bouncers but had dealt with them effectively in my opinion and so I had no reason to warn Donald.

3) Out, stumped. Interestingly, you would give the wicket here specifically because he was wearing a cap – had he been wearing a helmet the wicket would not have been awarded. Helmets are treated differently in the laws from caps and a wicket cannot be obtained from a direct deflection off a helmet for a catch. Equally for stumpings and run-outs from a helmet deflection, there must be a further interception by a fielder.

Learie Constantine

Full name: Baron Learie Nicholas Constantine
Date of birth: September 21, 1901
Major teams: West Indies, Barbados, Trinidad

Tests: 18	High Score: 90
Ave: 19.24	Wickets: 58
Centuries: 0	Bowling ave: 30.10
Fifties: 4	BBI: 5-75 BBM: 9-122

Learie Constantine was a true all-rounder: a fast bowler, dashing batsman and peerless fielder. He was first selected by West Indies for his astounding cover fielding, but soon proved himself to be a genuine quick bowler and an unorthodox but effective batsman. In 1930 he bowled the Windies to victory over England, their first Test triumph. But Test cricket never saw him at his best. Many of his finest performances were reserved for the town of Nelson in the Lancashire Cricket League.

Constantine's importance was not confined to cricket. He became an important campaigner for independence in the Caribbean and, during his time in England, massively raised the esteem in which his countrymen were held. On his return to Trinidad he became a cabinet minister and High Commisioner. In 1969 he was made Baron Constantine. He died in 1971.

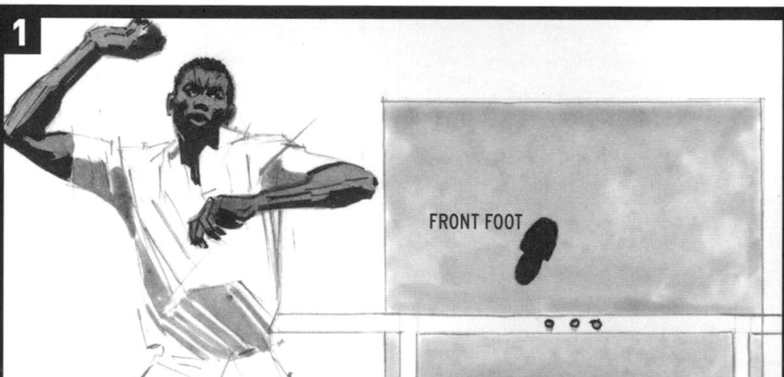
1
FRONT FOOT
Of the three illustrations, can you correctly identify which are legal deliveries and which are no balls – and why?

Answers

1) No ball. Because no part of the front foot is behind the popping crease.

2) Legal delivery. Although the front foot is outside the return crease, part of it is behind the popping crease and the law allows that. The former West Indies bowler Colin Croft used to bowl like this, contorting his body in the delivery. This eventually led to him developing back trouble, putting an end to his career as a fast bowler. He did bowl really quickly and caused further problems for batsmen because of the unusual and awkward angle from which he delivered his thunderbolts.

3) Legal delivery. Part of his foot landed behind the popping crease, even though it slid over afterwards – it's where the foot lands that counts. John Holder: Among some of the fearsome West Indies fast-bowlers, including Michael Holding, Curtly Ambrose, Andy Roberts and Malcolm Marshall, all of whom were certainly guilty of the occasional no-ball, Holding was the quickest I saw. He had the most beautifully athletic, graceful approach to the wicket. Seemingly gliding in from 40 yards, his run-up was so silent that Dickie Bird nicknamed him 'Whispering Death'. In a Test Match at Kensington Oval in Barbados he bowled an over to Geoffrey Boycott that was, for the people who witnessed it, one of the greatest, fastest, most hostile overs ever seen. The first few balls flashed past the bat and then his wicket was flattened. Truly sensational, especially given that Boycott was a player with such excellent technique, bags of grit, determination and concentration.

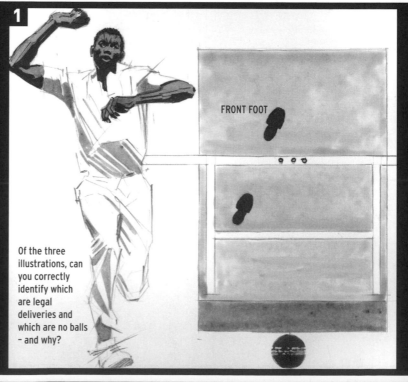

3

The wicketkeeper is standing up to the stumps for a slow bowler. The batsman steps out of the crease, goes for a big hit and edges the ball, which flies through and hits the keeper on his cap before dropping onto the stumps and removing the bails. The fielding side appeal for the stumping. What do you give?

Answers

1) Still give the batsman out. Regardless of whether it was the fifth or seventh ball of the over, the wicket stands. And the fact that your colleague said you miscounted does not mean he's correct – he may have miscounted himself – but whether you have made a mistake or not, any runs or wickets taken from an erroneous ball still count. Umpires usually have a pre-arrangement where they signal to each other either on the fourth or fifth ball of the over to confirm the number of balls bowled. If there's uncertainty they'd check with the scorers.

2) Continue with the procedure for dealing with dangerous and unfair bowling. Umpires are the sole judges of fair and unfair play. If you have judged the bowling unfair, taking into consideration the striker's skill, you must proceed to deal with the bowler, John Holder: In the 2000 season I witnessed a vintage confrontation between Allan Donald, playing for Warwickshire, and Justin Langer, for Middlesex, in a county match at Lord's. Donald opened the bowling at the pavilion end where I was standing. Langer drove the first ball savagely past mid-off for four and Donald, at

---

Curtly Ambrose

Full name: Curtly Elconn Lynwall Ambrose
Date of birth: September 21, 1963
Major teams: West Indies, Leeward Islands, Northamptonshire

Tests: 98	**ODIs:** 176
Ave: 12.40	**Ave:** 10.65
Fifties: 1	**Wickets:** 225
Wickets: 405	**Bowling ave:** 24.12
Bowling ave: 20.99	**BBM:** 5-17
BBI: 8-45 **BBM:** 11-84	

With 405 Test wickets, Curtly Ambrose is behind only his long-term ally Courtney Walsh in West Indian Test wicket takers. His tally is the 10th highest ever and, most impressively, only one player in the top 10 has played fewer Tests, and Ambrose possesses the lowest average – an astounding 20.99. Standing at six foot seven, bounce was always his strongest weapon, but when his early pace declined his accuracy and technique still made him lethal.

His most effective performance was probably a spell of seven for one, blowing away Australia at the WACA in 1993, although his greatest return was eight for 45 against England in 1990. His intimidating persona was enhanced by his famously taciturn manner, which he summed up with the motto, 'Curtly talk to no man'.

2

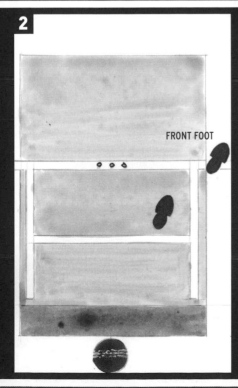

FRONT FOOT

3

FRONT FOOT
LANDS
THEN SLIDES
FORWARDS

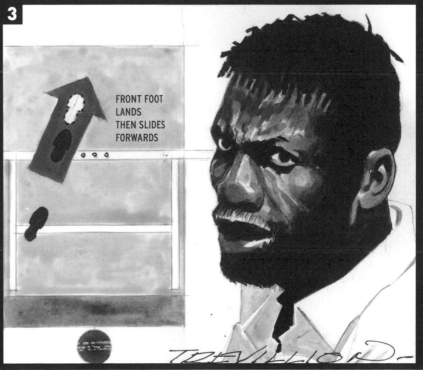

1

In a 50-over one-day match, the ball is changed after 34 overs, but the fielding captain refuses to use any of the balls offered to him because he deems them too soft. What do you do?

Imran Khan

Full name: Imran Khan Niazi
Date of birth: November 25, 1952
Major teams: Pakistan, Lahore, Worcestershire, PIA, Sussex

Tests: 88	ODIs: 175
Ave: 37.69	Ave: 33.41
Centuries: 6	Centuries: 1
Fifties: 18	Fifties: 19
High score: 136	High score: 102*
Wickets: 362	Wickets: 182
Bowling ave: 22.81	Bowling ave: 26.61
BBI: 8-58 BBM: 14-116	BBI: 6-14

A brilliant fast bowler, world-class all-rounder, socialite, politician and celebrity, Imran Khan inspired a generation of cricket fans from the subcontinent to take up pace bowling, and massively increased female interest in the sport. His bowling, often on the thankless pitches of Pakistan, was inspirational: on retirement he held the Test and ODI wicket-taking records for Pakistan. He started as a medium pacer but his speed increased to such an extent that he finished third, behind Jeff Thompson and Michael Holding, in a fast-bowling contest in 1978. His potency was enhanced by his mastery of yorkers and reverse swing.

Unlike Ian Botham or Kapil Dev, who were top all-rounders from the start, Imran was a slow starter and, initially, principally a bowler. He had to wait until his 30th Test to score his first century and he only passed 50 three times in his first 37. However, after this lean start he became a brilliant batsman, meriting selection for his run scoring alone. Having begun as a No8, he ended his career batting as high as No5 in Tests, from where he scored a fine 136 against Australia, and No3 in ODIs. His career ended, fittingly for a late bloomer, with its highlight: scoring 72 from No3 as he captained Pakistan to victory over England in the 1992 World Cup final.

2

At the end of the 79th over in a Test match, the umpire retrieves the new ball from the small pit in the outfield behind the wicketkeeper, but fails to close the lid properly. The next over, the batsman hits a straight drive and the ball ends up in the pit. Can the batsmen keep running until the ball is retrieved by the fielding side?

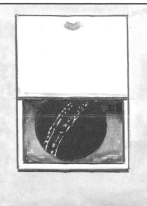

3

A bowler bowls his first ball of the match and the ball flies, unintentionally, very wide and would clearly be given as a wide ball. The batsman, however, quickly runs out to the ball, swings at it, takes a top edge and is caught. Is the ball a wide or is the batsman out, and at which point should you turn to signal your decision?

TREVILLION

Answers

1) If the captain continues to refuse to bowl with the balls on offer, there's nothing you can do – he'll forfeit the match because of a refusal to play. You need to warn him that this will happen and, if he still refuses, the match is awarded to the batting side. In the 2006 Test match at The Oval between England and Pakistan, Pakistan were accused of ball-tampering, the ball was changed and England were awarded five penalty runs. Pakistan refused to play and umpires Darrell Hair and Billy Doctrove awarded the match to England.

2) Yes, the batsmen can keep running until the ball is retrieved. This situation must be treated like 'lost ball'. The batsmen can run until a member of the fielding side shouts 'lost ball', at which point the striker will receive a minimum of six runs, or more, if they had already completed them.

3) Give the batsman out – once the striker moves and brings the ball within reach, it cannot be considered a wide. However, if the ball had slipped from the bowler's hand during the delivery, you would immediately call, and signal, dead ball and the batsman would have no right to strike the ball. Because of situations like this, where a potential wide becomes a wicket, you should never turn to signal to the scorers until, in your opinion, the ball is dead.

1 You are the square leg umpire. One batsman, currently the non-striker, has made his mark outside the crease. The batsman on strike calls an easy single: the non-striker strolls down the pitch and takes his stance at his mark but does not touch the crease to make the run. Do you
a) call one short, or
b) make no call?

2 The bowling side have chosen to continue with the old ball. It is soft, going out of shape and the stitching is unpicking – but it suits their slow bowling attack. The batsmen protest that it's unfair: both hard to hit and bouncing erratically. What do you do?

Answers

1) b) Make no call. The batsman didn't attempt to run short, so you can't call short run. If the fielding side had noticed he hadn't made good his ground and had put the wicket down at that end, you'd then have given the batsman out on appeal.

2) The batsmen cannot demand a new ball, but they can complain to you: the umpires are the sole judges of fair and unfair play. In this instance you should change the ball for one in a better condition.

3) Give the batsman out – but before you do so, check with the fielding captain if he wants the appeal to stand. This is a question where the spirit of cricket is important – the code of conduct which states that the game should be played with due respect to one's team-mates, opponents, umpires and the traditional values of the sport. Only if the fielding captain insists on the appeal standing should you give the striker out, run out. John Holder: The ODI at The Oval in 2008 between England and New Zealand proved the importance everyone places on playing within the spirit of the game. Ryan Sidebottom collided with an opposing batsman who fell; the wicket was broken and there was an appeal. Mark Benson asked Paul Collingwood if he wanted the appeal to stand, he said yes so the run-out was given. Collingwood later apologised.

Clive Lloyd

Full name: Clive Hubert Lloyd
Date of birth: August 31, 1944
Major teams: West Indies, British Guiana, Guyana, Lancashire

Tests: 110	ODIs: 87
Ave: 46.67	Ave: 39.54
Centuries: 19	Centuries: 1
Fifties: 39	Fifties: 11
High score: 242*	High score: 102

Tall and muscular, Clive Lloyd's instincts were to bludgeon. However, experience and necessity tempered his attacking instincts and he was often at his best when digging his team out of a hole. From his position in the middle-order he was an anchor for West Indies, though he could still destroy the best attacks when the situation demanded it. He was also a useful medium-pace bowler and a fine cover point and slip fielder.

His thick glasses and heavy bat were a fixture on the international scene for nearly 20 years and he became the first West Indian to win 100 caps. His greatest achievement was to usher in the era of West Indian dominance. As captain he presided over one of the greatest teams in history. He led by example, and took his country to a run of 26 Tests without defeat as well as two World Cup victories.

1 On a windy day the batsmen go for a quick single. A fielder collects the ball but, as he approaches the stumps to attempt a run out, the wind blows the bails off. Can he still claim a run out, and if so, how?

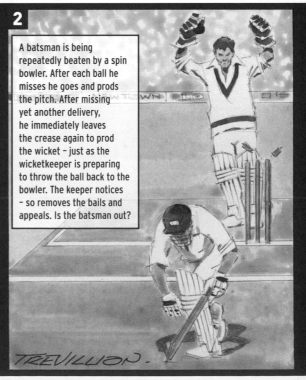

2 A batsman is being repeatedly beaten by a spin bowler. After each ball he misses he goes and prods the pitch. After missing yet another delivery, he immediately leaves the crease again to prod the wicket – just as the wicketkeeper is preparing to throw the ball back to the bowler. The keeper notices – so removes the bails and appeals. Is the batsman out?

3) He's out, lbw. When the bowler starts his run up, whatever stance the batsman is in determines off side and leg side. The fact that he switched stance during the bowler's approach makes no difference, as he would still be deemed right-handed. John Holder: There was a furore over Kevin Pietersen's similar shot against New Zealand at Durham the first time he tried this. Had he been dismissed attempting the shot, the press would have lambasted him for being arrogant and reckless. Mike Gatting was criticised for attempting a reverse sweep in the 1987 World Cup final and getting out in the process. He was blamed for England losing.

3

A batsman is hit on the pad. There's an appeal, but you give not out. The relieved batsman, in the process of un-velcroing his gloves, inadvertently steps out of his crease. A fielder picks up the ball, hits the stumps and appeals. What do you do?

Alan Knott

Full name: Alan Philip Eric Knott
Date of birth: April 9, 1946
Major teams: England, Kent, Tasmania

Tests: 95	ODIs: 20
Ct: 250 St: 19	Ct: 15 St: 1
Ave: 32.75	Ave: 20.00
Centuries: 5	Centuries: 0
Fifties: 30	Fifties: 1
High score: 135	High score: 50

One of the most talented wicketkeepers that England – and the world – has ever known, Alan Knott was nimble, athletic and technically excellent, though his true value was his reliability. The sight of him performing his trademark stretches during lulls in matches was a great boon to team-mates and fans alike. Early in his career he was kept out of the England team by Jim Parks, but soon his exemplary keeping and some useful fifties earned him a permanent place in Test side. Indeed, his batting was more than proficient, bring a total of five centuries and thirty fifties in his Test career. A stoic player, he focused on the sweep and the cut. His talent was recognised by Wisden in 1970, when they made him one of their five Cricketers of the Year.

His decision to join Kerry Packer's World Series in 1977 interrupted his international career for three years and when he returned he failed to quite recapture his previous form. But by then he'd done enough to ensure that he was Godfrey Evans' only rival for England's finest ever wicketkeeper.

3

A batsman tries to sweep a slow ball by changing guard and grip to that of a left-hander just as the ball is released. The ball strikes the pad and the bowler appeals for lbw. But replays show that the ball would have spun from outside the left-hander's leg stump to hit middle stump. Do you still consider the batsman right-handed and give him out, or is he reprieved because he changed stance?

Answers

1) Yes, he can claim a run-out by a) striking a stump out of the ground with the ball or b) pulling the stump out of the ground with the ball in the same hand.

2) Very likely. It's up to you when the ball is dead. There are times when the ball automatically goes dead – such as when a wicket falls, a boundary is scored, or over or time is called. But when the ball goes through to the keeper or to a fielder it is up to the umpires. You don't want the keeper to hold the ball indefinitely, nor do you want either batsman to leave their ground prematurely. To avoid messes like this, both batsmen should wait a few seconds, making it obvious that they have no intention of moving out too quickly. John Holder: I would give him out. A few years ago in a county match between Worcester and Notts, Mark Crawley was given out run out as non-striker. Richard Illingworth bowled a ball which went through to Steve Rhodes the keeper, who quickly threw the ball back to Illingworth. He broke the wicket at the bowler's end with Crawley out of his ground. Umpire Trevor Jesty had no hesitation in giving Crawley out, run out.

BOWLING AT THE BATSMAN'S BODY

By CRICKETER.

Never were Test matches more capricious than these; they are better than any tale. Not a move can be foreseen, not a step. Consider the play before lunch at Adelaide on Friday, and then the play before lunch on Saturday. England four wickets down in an hour and a half; England's greatest batsmen reduced to helplessness. Then, next morning, the Australian attack is held up and defied for an hour and a half by Hedley Verity, who, like a born Yorkshireman, proceeds to help himself, with colossal impertinence, to 45 in a Test match. Meanwhile Paynter of Lancashire uses his quick feet, dancing down the pitch to O'Reilly. Not a single wicket could Australia capture on Saturday before lunch. The English rally was glorious; character, good North of England toughness, conquered an evil situation. The total of 341 might well have made Woodfull sick with disillusion. "Why did the gods flatter us so greatly yesterday?" we can almost hear him saying. "Why this extreme humiliation?—Verity 45; many, many more runs than I, Heaven help me, can hope to make in Test matches nowadays."

The game's seesaw went dizzy again as soon as the Australians batted. And we can feel what a dramatic seesaw it is, hurtling the men on it now high, now low. On Saturday afternoon Larwood made the beautiful Adelaide wicket seem like a battlefield. Fury and smoke were in his work. Fingleton out straightway—then Bradman! He is obviously dismayed by Larwood; he ducks as the missiles fly about his head. Then Woodfull receives a blow over the heart. Poor Woodfull's face goes grey and old with pain. . . . And this is Adelaide the golden, the happy hunting ground of all good batsmen !

Bradman tries to hook Larwood and is caught in the accursed leg-trap. McCabe falls to the same brutal device —for we must be frank: it is brutal. Some day, if a cricketer gets killed by this body-bowling, we shall have an end of it. Bowling directed to the batsman's body, with the field packed on the leg side, puts the attack outside the range of half the batsman's means of retaliation: a fast rising ball, coming straight at the chest or heart, can only be countered by a stroke like a shield. And the leg-trap picks up the catch sent by a batsman saving his head, and his wicket. The morality of such bowling is open to question. It amounts to this: the attack is really directed not at Bradman a batsman who possesses strokes all round the wicket, but at Bradman a human being governed like all of us by the instinct for self-preservation. Fast bowlers of old, including McDonald and Gregory, pitched their bumpers in front of the batsmen, where they could see them; they did not systematically send along short kickers clean at the head and body.

Frankly, it does not seem cricket to me. And nobody in this country seems to realise yet how badly the Australian public is taking the English violence. The following from the excellent Sydney is significant :—"There is any doubt about the plan of England's fast bowlers. It is a head-and-body attack, persisted in there can be result—the maiming of batsmen. The introduction of this system of attack may have its effects. It can be stopped. Reprisals are not nice to speak our chaps won't take a bit this tour and another during of England two years he digging up someone who are physically as devastating of Voce, Larwood, and company of which has an ironic sound it does from the land which a ago produced Gregory and though, to be fair to the they are not objecting to such, but to the direction on the batsman's body, *on the wicket where a cricketer sibly make a scientific* Gregory and McDonald sel exploited leg-theory i us bowled to three or four sli part, if I were an Englan would prefer to lose a rubber by methods of attack a batsman think first of safety and prevented him f great technique, evolved game, and a contribution of it. Suppose we have a of fast leg-theory bow then will be the science a strokes of cricket ! On the

1 A captain wins the toss and is asked by his opposite number if he is to bat or field. The winning captain says he's had second thoughts and needs to go back and consult his players. The losing captain demands an immediate answer. What do you decide?

2 A batsman with a runner hits the ball into the deep and steps out of his crease to admire his shot. The runner and the non-striker complete three runs to win the game, but the batsman with the runner is still standing outside his crease when the wicket is broken. Would you give him out – and how many runs have been scored?

TREVILLION

Answers

1) Allow the winning captain to consult his players. The toss must be made no more than 30 minutes and no fewer than 15 minutes before the scheduled start of play. So the captain has the time available to make his decision.

You would give him out, run out, if the wicket at the wicketkeeper's end is legally broken. He was out of his crease on the third run and, when the injured batsman is striker, he must always remain in his ground while the ball is live or be liable to be run out, irrespective of where his runner is.

3) Not out. At the moment the ball passed the striker on the full above waist height, you or your colleague will have called and signalled no ball: this is an illegal delivery. The fact that it then went on to cross the boundary means that five no-balls are awarded to the batting side and the bowler will receive a first and final warning for dangerous and unfair bowling. If, in your opinion, it was a deliberate act, then in addition to the no ball, you can ban the bowler immediately for the remainder of that innings, and report him to the authorities.

Harold Larwood

Full name: Harold Larwood
Date of birth: November 14, 1904
Major teams: England,
Nottinghamshire

Tests: 21
Ave: 19.40
Fifties: 2
High score: 98
Wickets: 78
Bowling ave: 28.35
BBI: 6-32 BBM: 10-124

One of England's greatest fast bowlers, Larwood was an accurate and fearsome bowler with a classical action and side-on delivery. He was particularly rapid for his era, and his peers maintained that he bowled at speeds of over 90mph. He made his England debut in 1926 but didn't secure his place until 1928, when he claimed 17 wickets against Australia. However, his career was to be defined, overshadowed and, ultimately, ended by the Bodyline controversy.

Don Bradman had so dominated the 1930 Ashes – scoring a world record 974 runs – that the England hierarchy decided that a plan had to be devised to nullify him for the 1932-33 series. Douglas Jardine, England's captain (see page 43), formulated a plan he dubbed 'leg theory': bowling the ball on leg stump so that it jumped into the body of the batsman, and packing the leg side field with close catchers. Larwood was the principal exponent of the plan. And it worked, with Bradman's average cut to 56 and Larwood taking 33 wickets at 19.51. However it was hugely controversial, sparking diplomatic incidents. Such was the furore that the MCC demanded Larwood apologise to the Australian Board and players. Larwood maintained that he was simply following the tactics set by his captain, refused and was never again picked for England. He died in 1995.

3

A fast bowler fires a full toss down the pitch at chest height. The batsman steps back out of the way, but the ball dips suddenly, strikes the top of the stumps, dislodges the bails and flies on and over the boundary for four. The bowler appeals. What is your decision?

1

A batsman reaches his century and, to allow other members on his team some time in the middle, retires. Wickets quickly fall and the star batsman wishes to return. The opposing captain objects. What do you do?

match will be restarted from the beginning.
John Holder: The 1998 Jamaica Test between West Indies and England at Sabina Park, on a newly laid pitch, was abandoned by the umpires because the surface was dangerous. England were asked to bat first with Atherton and Stewart facing Ambrose and Walsh. It was frightening watching as some balls shot along the ground and others whizzed past their nostrils or struck them at speeds of over 90mph. There was a real danger of serious injury to both batsmen, so the umpires correctly abandoned the match with England 17 for three. Steve Bucknor, a Jamaican, was one of the umpires and, though partisan supporters criticised him, he was right.

3) Out. The batsman has no say in the matter. The equipment may very well be all that is available and if that's the case that's what you make use of. There are times when, because it's very windy for example, the bails are dispensed with altogether. The fielding side could also say that the wicket was too small, which would be a farcical situation. In a professional match this would never happen as umpires are responsible for the running of the game and part of their pre-match duties is to check that the available equipment meets the legal standards. There are always adequate supplies of equipment.

Derek Randall

Full name: Derek William Randall
Date of birth: February 24, 1951
Major teams: England, Nottinghamshire, Suffolk

Tests: 47
Ave: 33.37
Centuries: 7
Fifties: 12
High score: 174

ODIs: 49
Ave: 26.67
Fifties: 5
High score: 88

Derek Randall's reputation far exceeds his statistics. He ended his career with disappointing averages of 33.37 and 26.67 in Test and ODIs respectively, but it was his eccentrically stylish use of the bat that won him plaudits, despite a lack of consistency. His greatest innings were two massive knocks against Australia: a 174 in the 1977 Centenary Test and a 150 at Sydney in 1979.

But even more spectacular than his batting was his fielding. A phenomenal cover fielder, agile and fast, he pulled off several spectacular catches and was also known for effecting run outs. These qualities made him a popular figure, earning him the nickname 'Arkle' after the racehorse, as did his joyful, eccentric manner: doffing his hat to a Dennis Lillee bouncer, for example.

The batsman clubs a ball high towards the boundary, a fielder in the deep jumps towards the ball for a high catch and, while in the air, his cap falls off and lands inside the boundary on the ground behind him. He manages to put a hand on the ball but cannot control it and it falls to the ground. He turns around and sees that the ball has landed in his cap without touching the ground. He picks it up and immediately appeals. What do you give?

2 On the first morning of a match the light is good, but the pitch appears to be in a doubtful condition. However, both teams want to play. It's a championship decider. Quickly the side batting are in trouble, with players struck regularly by balls due to the bounce being highly inconsistent. What do you do?

3 You're at the bowler's end. A batsman is bowled, the ball clipping the off bail while leaving the leg bail in place. The defeated batsman looks at his broken wicket and says the surviving bail is too big and if it had been the correct size, the ball wouldn't have made contact. The batsman is right. Your colleague hasn't checked the size of the bails – they're clearly too big. What do you do?

Answers

1) Out. If he leaves the field of play without being dismissed or injured he is ruled to be 'retired out'. A batsman can't just walk off the field and return to bat when it suits him. Early in the season in non-championship matches against the universities, county batsmen who've made big scores retire to give other batsmen match practice. In every instance they are recorded as retired out.

2) If, in the umpire's opinion, the pitch is a dangerous one and there's a real risk of injury to the batsmen they will, after consulting with both captains and the ground authority, abandon the match. If it's possible, an attempt will be made to prepare another pitch on the square and the

Basil D'Oliveira

Full name: Basil Lewis D'Oliveira
Date of birth: October 4, 1931
Major teams: England, Worcestershire

Tests: 44   Wickets: 47
Ave: 40.06   Bowling ave: 39.55
Centuries: 5   BBI: 3-46
Fifties: 15   BBM: 5-62
High score: 158

Basil D'Oliveira's England career is often overshadowed by the circumstances that led him to having an England career in the first place. Classified as 'Cape coloured' by South Africa's apartheid regime, he was barred from playing for his home country and emigrated to England in 1960. By 1966 he attained British citizenship, and was selected for his first Test. His presence in the England team caused a diplomatic incident when he was selected for a tour of South Africa, resulting in its cancellation by South African Prime Minister BJ Vorster. It was one of the decisive events leading to the boycott of South African sport.

An all-rounder, D'Oliveira, in his 44 Tests for England, achieved a batting average of 40.06. As a bowler he took 551 wickets for Worcestershire at 27.45.

Answer

Not out. For the catch to count the ball would have had to lodge in the fielder's clothing. John Holder: I remember seeing the former Notts expert short-leg fielder Basharat Hassan catch Roger Knight, the former Surrey captain, in this way. Knight clipped a leg stump half volley straight into Basharat's midriff, where it lodged in his shirt. In this case, however, the ball is deemed to have landed on the ground – you wouldn't award penalty runs because the cap fell off accidentally. Had it been done deliberately to stop the ball, five penalty runs would be awarded to the batting side. The ball isn't dead, though, and the batsmen may continue running until it is thrown in to either end.

KEY MOMENT

Ricky Ponting

Australia v England
Ashes 1st Test, Brisbane,
23-27 November 2006
First innings: 196 runs, 464
mins, 319 balls, 24 fours.
Second innings: 60* runs,
131 mins, 85 balls, 4 fours.
Australia won by 277 runs

Ricky Ponting was thoroughly castigated for his role in Australia's failed Ashes campaign in 2005: poor captaincy decisions, embarrassing losses of composure and the defeat itself tarnishing his reputation. His job as captain was probably dependent on Australia reclaiming the Ashes at the first attempt.

Having won the toss, he chose to bat on an even pitch and his team were immediately handed the initiative by Steve Harmison's opening salvo – a ball that was so wide it went straight to Andrew Flintoff at second slip. Ponting, once in, imposed himself. He batted without incident and was only threatened once when a missed sweep off a straight ball from Ashley Giles elicited a close lbw shout as he passed 100.

On the second day, England's toil continued, with Ponting and Michael Hussey compiling a partnership of 209. Ponting was finally dismissed by Matthew Hoggard for 196, a score that edged him ahead of Graham Gooch to become the seventh highest Test run scorer. His century was his 32nd, taking him level with Steve Waugh as Australia's leading Test century-maker. More importantly, it had won the match and, such was the dominance of the victory, seemed to make the reclamation of the Ashes an inevitability. Full biography, page 20

1

A batsman hits the ball straight down the pitch. The bowler attempts a catch, but only succeeds in deflecting the ball. At the other end, the non-striking batsman, out of his ground, suddenly realises that the ball will hit his wicket and run him out, so he instinctively sticks out his bat. He connects and the ball bounces off past the fielders, over the boundary ropes. What is your decision?

1

A batsman hits a high ball over the boundary. A fielder runs off the pitch and, as the ball approaches him, he jumps off the ground and knocks the ball back into the field of play while in mid-air – straight into the hands of a team-mate to catch. What do you give?

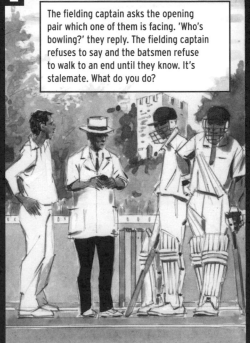

2

The fielding captain asks the opening pair which one of them is facing. 'Who's bowling?' they reply. The fielding captain refuses to say and the batsmen refuse to walk to an end until they know. It's stalemate. What do you do?

Answers

1) **Out** – caught on appeal. Because the ball didn't touch the boundary rope, or fence, or the ground beyond, and no part of the fielder's person was in contact with, or grounded over, the fence or rope – it counts as a legitimate catch rather than a boundary.

2) It's up to the bowler or the fielding captain to decide who starts the bowling, and from which end. In this case the fielding captain is engaging in gamesmanship so you should warn him for time-wasting. If he persists in holding play up you would warn him that his actions could lead to him being considered as refusing to play and so forfeiting the match, after which he could be reported to the governing body and face a further penalty. Once the bowler and end have been designated, whichever batsman is to face the first ball should proceed to the appropriate end as soon as possible.

3) **Out.** This is a very unfortunate incident but he's run out on appeal. The ball colliding with the bat is entirely coincidental and, unless the fielding captain was very generous and withdrew the appeal, the unlucky batsman would have to go.

2 A batsman arrives at the wicket with the handle on his bat almost twice the standard thickness. There are at least five additional wrap-rounds. The wicketkeeper calls it to your attention and insists it's now an illegal power weapon. What is your decision?

3 A bouncer hits the top of the batsman's helmet and the ball goes straight up, high into the air. As it drops, the batsman, unsettled by the blow, promptly dispatches the dropping ball over the boundary ropes. Is it a six?

Answers

1) The bowler's end umpire must decide whether or not the non-striker deliberately intercepted the ball. If he did, then, on appeal, give him out for obstruction. On no account can runs be scored for an illegal action. This is a situation where the umpires would confer if the bowler's end umpire has any doubts about the legality of the interception.

2) There's no restriction on the thickness of the bat handle. A player can have as many rubbers on it as he likes. John Holder, Clive Lloyd, a very tall man with big hands, used to have several rubbers on his bat handle, which a player with smaller hands couldn't grip. The important thing is that the player feels comfortable with his playing equipment.

3) The helmet is part of the batsman's person and, as the ball has already struck it, he cannot then strike the ball again. If he does so, he will be given out 'hit the ball twice', on appeal. He can only legally hit the ball twice in defending his wicket after it has come off his bat or person and before it has been touched by a fielder – although he can't take his hand off the bat and deflect the ball away with that hand.

Garry Sobers

Full name: Sir Garfield St Auburn Sobers
Date of birth: July 28, 1936
Major teams: West Indies, Barbados, Nottinghamshire, South Australia

Tests: 93
Ave: 57.78
Centuries: 26
Fifties: 30
High score: 365*
Wickets: 235
Bowling ave: 34.03
BBI: 6-73 BBM: 8-80

When Wisden organised a vote for their five Cricketers of the Twentieth Century, two votes were considered a given, so obvious was it that Don Bradman and Garry Sobers would be included on everyone's lists. The greatest all-rounder in the history of the game, Sobers was a truly natural sportsman who, aside from cricket, also played football, table tennis, golf, dominoes and basketball for Barbados. As a cricketer he started principally as a bowler and showed a genius for variation, being able to bowl medium pace, left-arm orthodox and left-arm chinaman. He collected 235 Test wickets.

It was as a batsman, however, that he ultimately excelled, amassing a total of 8,032 Test runs and 26 centuries. An elegant player with impeccable timing, he was the master of seeing the ball early and playing it late. In 1958 this technique took him to 365 not out in an innings against Pakistan, a Test record that stood for 36 years and remains the highest first century ever scored in Tests. He could also be explosive: he was the first batsman to score six sixes in an over in first-class cricket, against the unfortunate Malcolm Nash when playing for Nottinghamshire. As a captain he led West Indies in 39 Tests and inspired the process through which the Windies became a great side.

3 A batsman has just run a quick single and reaches forward to ground his bat inside the crease. A fielder throws the ball at the stumps but it hits the bat, and knocks it out of the batsman's hands. The ball is then deflected onto the stumps. The batsman is still outside his crease and no longer holding his bat when the fielding side appeals. What do you give?

1

A batsman drives the ball through the air. It strikes the top of the stumps at the non-striker's end without being touched by a fielder, then ricochets off the stumps without removing the bails and the ball is caught. The fielder appeals. What is your decision?

TREVILLION

Kapil Dev

Full name: Kapildev Ramlal Nikhanj
Date of birth: January 6, 1959
Major teams: India, Haryana, Northamptonshire, Worcestershire

Tests: 131	ODIs: 225
Ave: 31.05	Ave: 23.79
Centuries: 8	Centuries: 1
Fifties: 27	Fifties: 14
High score: 163	High score: 175*
Wickets: 434	Wickets: 253
Bowling ave: 29.64	Bowling ave: 27.45
BBI: 9-83	BBM: 5-43
BBM: 11-146	

Along with Ian Botham, Imran Khan and Sir Richard Hadlee, Kapil Dev was one of the great all-rounders of the 1980s. As a bowler he wasn't terrifically fast, but he possessed great accuracy, stamina and a wonderfully controlled away-swinger. After a knee injury in 1984 required surgery, the pace and potency of his bowling decreased, but he retained the ability to take wickets, with his inswinging yorker still brilliant at cleaning up tailenders. By the time he retired he'd taken a world record 434 Test wickets, while his ODI tally of 253 wickets remained a record until 1994.

His batting, not the most technical, was powerful, explosive and of a high enough quality to produce eight Test centuries. He's the only player to have achieved the all-rounders' double of 4,000 Test runs and 400 Test wickets. He captained India to the World Cup title in 1983, beating the mighty West Indies by 43 runs. Kapil himself underperformed in that match – scoring 15 runs and taking a solitary wicket – but, against Zimbabwe earlier in the tournament, he had hit 175 from just 138 balls. It was, at the time, the highest score in ODIs. Such is his stature and legacy in his home country that in 2002 he was voted India's Cricketer of the Century.

2

Six runs are required to win off the last ball. The batsman goes for it, but a fielder on the boundary is under the ball. He drops it, but manages to run the batsman out. You give the man out, but then you notice on the big screen replay that the fielder actually had his foot on the boundary rope as he dropped the catch. The batsman points at the screen and protests. Can you reverse your decision and give a six, thus awarding the match to the batting side?

3

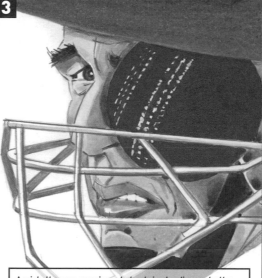

A wicketkeeper, wearing a helmet, is standing up to the stumps. The batsman edges the ball and it sticks between the grille and the top of the helmet. The keeper pulls the ball out and appeals. The batsman stands his ground. What do you give?

Answers

1) The batsman is out caught. Although the ball has hit the stumps at the bowler's end, it hasn't touched the ground, so the catch is a good one.

2) Yes, reverse your decision, give the six and award the game to the batting side. An umpire is always entitled, after a big screen replay, to change his decision. In this case, because the fielder made contact with the rope, you should signal a six. But you should also deal with the batsman: he protested about your original decision, and he can be charged with dissent, which could mean a fine. It's also important to bear in mind that in situations like this you can only reverse a decision and call a batsman back if he hasn't already left the field of play.

3) Not out. When the ball lodged in the keeper's helmet it became automatically dead: the striker can't be dismissed. A helmet worn by any member of the fielding side is treated differently from one worn by a batsman. Had the ball deflected from the striker's bat on to his helmet and was then caught directly by a member of the fielding side, he'd be out on appeal.

Mike Gatting

Full name: Michael William Gatting
Date of birth: June 6, 1957
Major teams: England, Middlesex

Tests: 79   ODIs: 92
Ave: 35.55   Ave: 29.50
Centuries: 10   Centuries: 1
Fifties: 21   Fifties: 9
High score: 207   High score: 115*

For a player who captained his country in 23 Tests and scored 10 Test centuries, it's perhaps unjust that Mike Gatting's career is remembered principally for three moments of infamy: being the hapless victim of Shane Warne's Ball of the Century; a vicious argument with Pakistani umpire Shakoor Rana; and his dismissal as England captain for an alleged escapade with a barmaid.

A natural cricketer who failed to exploit his talents to the full on the international stage, Gatting was a powerful batsman, renowned for his drives through extra cover, and had a rare talent for playing spinners. He made his debut in 1978 but started slowly, failing to make a Test century until 1985. But subsequently he thrived, with his personal highlight occurring soon afterwards when he hit a double century against India in Madras (now Chennai). He was appointed captain in 1986 and, against the odds, won the Ashes in 1986-87. The rest of his captaincy was only a limited success, though, and following the Rana and barmaid affairs he was dismissed. A rebel tour to South Africa followed, putting paid to his chances of reclaiming the captaincy.

1

A short ball is missed by the batsman while he tries to hook. It hits his visor – and bizarrely he claims his false teeth flew out and dislodged a bail before he completed his stroke. But you then find his false teeth lying beside the bail. What do you give?

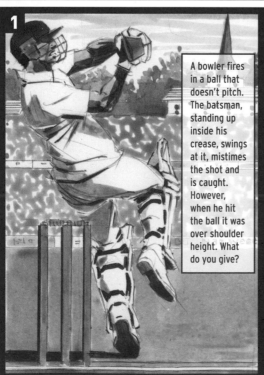

1

A bowler fires in a ball that doesn't pitch. The batsman, standing up inside his crease, swings at it, mistimes the shot and is caught. However, when he hit the ball it was over shoulder height. What do you give?

2

In the last over, with three runs needed for a win, the batsman stands well out of his crease to a medium-paced bowler. He misses the ball, the wicketkeeper collects it and throws it at the stumps. It breaks the wicket and the keeper appeals. Is the batsman run out or stumped?

2

A batsman edges the ball to the wicketkeeper who immediately appeals and the batsman walks. However the keeper drops the ball before he has it completely under control. He realises the batsman has walked, scoops the ball up, removes the bails and appeals. What do you give?

3

A bowler, fielding in the deep, leaves his drinks bottle just within the boundary as he steps up to bowl the next over. On returning to his fielding position he moves to take a catch, but while doing so, slips and makes contact with his drink bottle which is up against the boundary rope. The ball then lands on the drinks bottle, bounces into the air and he catches it. What do you give?

Answers

1) Out – hit wicket. The false teeth are treated as a part of his person, the same as if he'd trodden on the wicket while playing a stroke, or if his cap had broken the wicket.

2) Not out. If, in the umpire's opinion, the batsman has left his ground under a misapprehension (in this case thinking he was out, when he was not), dead ball will be called and the batsman will not be dismissed.

3) Not out and, because the ball hit the bottle, five penalty runs must be awarded. Even though the fielder was in contact with the bottle, which then touched the boundary rope, you wouldn't award four runs because no part of his actual person was in contact with, or was grounded over, the boundary line.

Barry Richards

Full name: Barry Anderson Richards
Date of birth: July 21, 1945
Major teams: South Africa, Gloucestershire, Hampshire, Natal, South Australia, Transvaal

Tests: 4
Ave: 72.57
Centuries: 2
Fifties: 2
High score: 140

Barry Richards arrived on the scene just as South Africa was emerging as a major cricketing nation. But players such as Richards, Graeme Pollock and Mike Procter were denied the chance to elevate their country, and themselves, into sporting greatness by apartheid, and the resultant banishment of South Africa from international cricket from 1970 to 1991. Richards was a significant loss to world cricket: a wonderfully fluid opening batsman with an exquisite technique, he scored two centuries in just four Tests, including a brilliant 140 against Australia in 1970.

Shunted from his rightful place on the international stage by politics, Richards plied his trade in county cricket, Australian grade cricket and, ultimately, in Kerry Packer's World Series Cricket. He had particular success at Hampshire, where he formed a memorable opening partnership with West Indies' Gordon Greenidge. Unfortunately, Richards' Test average of 72.27 isn't counted in lists of highest averages as he failed to play the requisite number of Test innings. However, while his average was perhaps inflated by the shortness of his career, a first-class average of over 54 is proof of his exceptional ability.

3

The captain of the home team comes up to you and tells you he has 13 players. He can't decide on which two players to leave out and the visiting team agree to play 13-a-side. Do you allow this?

Answers

1) Immediately call 'no ball' – the batsman is not out. Any ball that passes on the full over shoulder height is a no ball. If the umpire thought it was accidental, he'd give the bowler a first and final warning for dangerous and unfair bowling. If it was deemed to be deliberate the bowler would be removed from the attack immediately and wouldn't be allowed to bowl again that innings.

2) He's out stumped. He's not out run out because he wasn't attempting a run. The wicketkeeper doesn't have to have the ball in his gloves to stump a batsman: throwing it at the wicket will suffice.

3) Yes, the team can bat with as many players as they like, but only 11 are allowed to field at any one time.

1 A wicketkeeper throws off his glove and chases after a ball that has gone into the outfield. He picks it up and throws at the stumps while the batsmen run. A slip fielder puts on the discarded glove, catches the ball, whips off the bails and appeals. What is your decision?

TREVILLION-I

KEY MOMENT

Kevin Pietersen

England v Australia
Fifth Ashes Test, The Oval,
8-12 September 2005
First innings: 14 runs, 30 mins, 25 balls, 2 fours.
Second innings: 158 runs, 285 mins, 187 balls, 15 fours, 7 sixes.
Match drawn

The first Test of of the 2005 Ashes was Kevin Pietersen's debut: he hit 57 and 64 not out – becoming the fourth England player to top score in both innings on his debut – and proved that he wouldn't be intimidated by the Australia attack. Having fallen for 14 in his first innings of the final Ashes test at The Oval, Pietersen began his second with England in a precarious position and with the crowd fearing the traditional collapse.

England needed a draw to reclaim the Ashes: most batsmen would have dropped anchor, but Pietersen opted to counter-attack. He started in cavalier fashion, dropped three times early on. Shane Warne dropped a dolly off him when he was on 15; the next over the spinner was slog-swept for two sixes. After lunch, however, Pietersen played a scintillating innings, subduing Warne and savaging Brett Lee's 95mph barrage, pulling him three times over the square boundary. A baseball swipe that whistled by the umpire for four was typically audacious, and KP's maiden century was brought up with an extra-cover drive to the boundary. His innings was ended by a Glenn McGrath leg-cutter on 158, but by then the urn was England's. Pietersen had played one of the all-time great Ashes innings. Full biography, page 14

78

2

A batsman receives a ball pitched well up, just wide of the off stump, which he hits, striking a fielder full on his helmet. It's caught by first slip without touching the ground. Would the batsman be out on appeal?

3

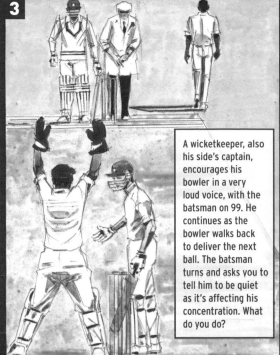

A wicketkeeper, also his side's captain, encourages his bowler in a very loud voice, with the batsman on 99. He continues as the bowler walks back to deliver the next ball. The batsman turns and asks you to tell him to be quiet as it's affecting his concentration. What do you do?

Answers

1) You should award five penalty runs to the batting side for illegal fielding, plus whatever runs have been completed. The wicketkeeper is the only member of the fielding side who can field a live ball with a glove.

2) A batsman cannot be out caught off a ball that has struck a fielder's helmet. However, he can be dismissed if the ball strikes a fielder's cap. The helmet allows the fielder to get closer to the batsman than normal, so the law doesn't allow there to be a catch directly from the helmet. Similarly, a batsman cannot be run out from a ball that rebounds off a fielder's helmet on to the stumps.

3) You may regard the wicketkeeper's behaviour as a deliberate attempt to distract the batsman. You should warn him and, if there's a repeat, award five penalty runs to the batting side, then report the incident to the relevant cricket authority.

1 A player is bowled first ball of the over – but his captain rushes to complain that you miscounted the balls bowled in the previous over. You realise he's right. Is the batsman out or do you go back and complete the previous over?

2 A wicketkeeper/captain has his field spread well out with one slip in an effort to stop the opposition from winning in fading light. After each ball bowled, the wicketkeeper has long discussions with his slip fielder. The batsman complains that the wicketkeeper is deliberately wasting time. What action do you take?

TREVILLION.

KEY MOMENT

Muttiah Muralitharan

England v Sri Lanka
The Oval,
27–31 August 1998
First innings: 7-155
Second innings: 9-65
Sri Lanka beat
England by 10 wickets

In a one-off match against England at The Oval, Murali took seven for 155 and nine for 65 to give Sri Lanka their first ever Test victory in England. His figures of 16 for 220 remain the fifth greatest match figures and his second-innings return is the ninth-greatest innings figures ever.

In England's first innings, Murali was superb, taking seven wickets. But England managed to put up a fight, with Graeme Hick and John Crawley scoring 107 and 156 not out respectively. But in the second innings,

Murali's dominance was complete – Mark Ramprakash's 42 was England's highest score and three batsmen were dismissed for 0. They simply couldn't counter the Sri Lankan's array of deliveries, his control, his guile: a vicious leg-break bowled round the wicket to left-hander Mark Butcher ended in a stumping; a faster ball, turning half a foot to leg, trapped Hick lbw; Crawley was bowled between bat and pad with a ball that pitched on off and hit leg. The wicket of Ben Hollioake, trapped with a top-spinning yorker for 0, was Murali's 200th wicket.

Although he failed to equal the efforts of Jim Laker and Anil Kumble, who both took all 10 wickets in a Test innings, he was the only wicket taker in England's second innings, as Alec Stewart was run out. It was one of the great bowling performances and earned, almost single-handedly, Sri Lanka a famous victory.

Full biography, page 18.

Answers

1) Ask the bowler to remove the plaster. Some feel that having the plaster on the finger of the bowling hand could give him a better grip on the ball – though in reality it reduces grip. Either way, the law allows it only if the batsman doesn't object. John Holder: Whenever a bowler asks me if it's OK to have a plaster on his bowling hand, I always ask the batsmen if they have any objection.

2) Allow the fielder to remain where he is. The batting captain has no say as to who can substitute or where they can field (except a sub cannot keep wicket). John Holder: At Trent Bridge in the Ashes Test in 2005, Gary Pratt, the ex-Durham batsman and a brilliant fielder, was fielding substitute for England and ran out Ricky Ponting at a crucial stage of the match. Ponting complained, unsuccessfully, that England had used such an outstanding fielder as twelfth man. He hadn't known how good a fielder Pratt was when he went for the run, but the law on no substitutes had not been transgressed.

3) The striker is out caught on appeal, because although the ball had hit the wicket and broken it, it had still not struck the ground before it was caught.

1 A spinner, fielding his own bowling, splits his forefinger. He leaves the field for treatment and returns with a plaster covering two thirds of the damaged finger. When he comes back on to bowl, the batsman insists the plaster gives additional leverage when he spins the ball and demands the plaster is removed. What is your decision?

3

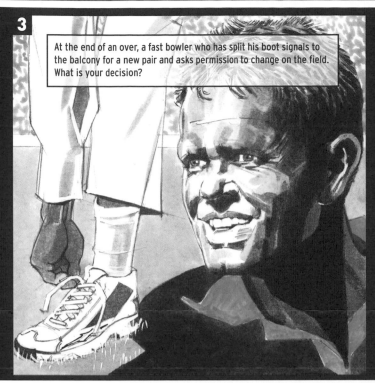

At the end of an over, a fast bowler who has split his boot signals to the balcony for a new pair and asks permission to change on the field. What is your decision?

Shaun Pollock

Full name: Shaun Maclean Pollock
Date of birth: June 16, 1973
Major teams: South Africa, Natal, Warwickshire, Durham, Mumbai Indians

Tests: 108
Ave: 32.31
Centuries: 2
Fifties: 16
High score: 111
Wickets: 421
Bowling ave: 23.11
BBI: 7-87 BBM: 10-147

ODIs: 303
Ave: 26.45
Centuries: 1
Fifties: 14
High score: 130
Wickets: 393
Bowling ave: 24.50
BBI: 6-35

Answers

1) The batsman is out – the captain has no right to object. If an umpire miscounts the number of balls bowled, the over stands. John Holder: In the 1990 Old Trafford Test against India, John Hampshire and I were the umpires. During an over we twice ran off for rain. After the second break we'd lost count of the number of balls bowled. We both had four coins left in our pockets – which we use for counting each delivery - so we allowed four more deliveries. It resulted in an eight-ball over.

2) Warn him: this is blatant time-wasting. If he persists, award five penalty runs to the batting side. John Holder: In the Karachi Test during England's 2001-02 tour to Pakistan, with England in a strong position to knock off the runs in near darkness, Pakistan captain Moin Khan repeatedly walked 90 yards to talk to Waqar Younis, wasting time. Then, as it got darker, he complained to the umpires about the light. The umpires ignored him, kept play going and England won.

3) Deny him permission: players must leave the field to change. No substitute is allowed.

Son of Peter and nephew of Graeme, both Test cricketers, Shaun Pollock was one of the great players of his generation: a world-class fast bowler and one of the most effective lower-order batsmen ever. He started as a fire-and-brimstone bowler, concentrating on speed and bouncers. As he matured, however, he focused on accuracy. His dedication to line and length, and his ability to swing the ball both ways, brought him 421 Test wickets – more than any other South African. He also proved a highly effective lower-order batsman, both hard-hitting and stubborn, and is one of only six players to have scored over 3,000 runs and taken over 300 wickets in Test cricket.

Pollock made his debut against England in 1995 and went on to play in 108 Tests and make 303 ODI appearances, a record for his country. He had many career triumphs, including taking seven for 87 against Australia – just one of 16 five-wicket hauls – and centuries, both scored at No9, against Sri Lanka and West Indies. He assumed the captaincy in 2000 in the aftermath of the Hansie Cronje scandal but failed to lift a shell-shocked team, losing heavily to Australia before exiting the 2002 World Cup in embarrassing circumstances. His pace having declined, he retired from international cricket in 2008.

2

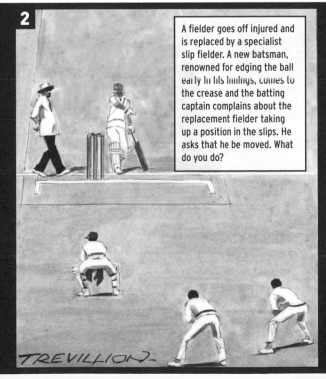

A fielder goes off injured and is replaced by a specialist slip fielder. A new batsman, renowned for edging the ball early in his innings, comes to the crease and the batting captain complains about the replacement fielder taking up a position in the slips. He asks that he be moved. What do you do?

TREVILLION

3

A batsman hammers the ball straight back through the air down the wicket. It breaks the middle stump, rebounds into the bowler's chest and flies into the air for the bowler, ignoring the pain, to make the catch and appeal. The batsman insists he's not out because the ball was dead when the wicket was broken. What is your decision?

Alastair Cook

Full name: Alastair Nathan Cook
Date of Birth: December 25, 1984
Teams: England, Essex

Tests: 34	ODIs: 23
Ave: 42.88	Ave: 30.52
Centuries: 7	Centuries: 1
Fifties: 14	Fifties: 3
High score: 127	High score: 102

For a batsman whose style is based on the old-fashioned disciplines of patience and accumulation, Alastair Cook has done everything in a hurry. At the age of 21 years and 69 days he became the youngest England player to score a century since 1951, at 22 he became the youngest player to score 2,000 Test runs for England and, in July 2007, he became the only England player to score seven centuries before the age of 23. He had owed his international debut to the misfortune of others – Michael Vaughan's injury and Marcus Trescothick's illness – but immediately showed international class, scoring 60 and 104 not out against India.

Cook often plays like a cricketer from a bygone era: watchful and phlegmatic, his technique is orthodox and simple, playing particularly off the back foot. The Australians exposed a weakness outside the off stump in the 2006-07 Ashes, but he still hit a fine 116 at Perth. His selection for the one-dayers surprised many, as did his ability to adapt to a faster tempo; but, as the improvements in his fielding have demonstrated, Cook is a player with a determination to develop. Earmarked as a future England captain, he has the time and the talent to break many more England batting records.

1

A big-hitting batsman, who has been blasting the ball repeatedly out of the ground, gives the ball another almighty whack. The ball can't take it any more – it suddenly splits in two. One half shatters the wicket at the bowler's end, with the non-striking batsman out of his crease. The other half flies into the slips and is caught, provoking simultaneous appeals for both incidents. Which batsman is out?

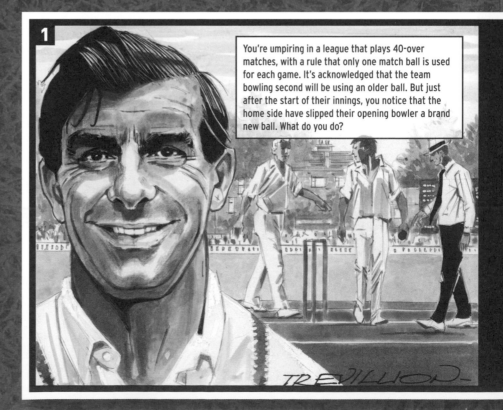

1

You're umpiring in a league that plays 40-over matches, with a rule that only one match ball is used for each game. It's acknowledged that the team bowling second will be using an older ball. But just after the start of their innings, you notice that the home side have slipped their opening bowler a brand new ball. What do you do?

2

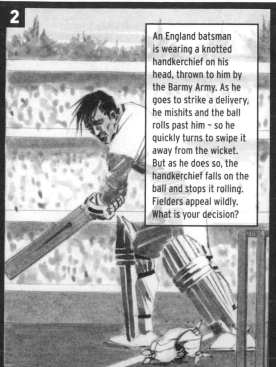

An England batsman is wearing a knotted handkerchief on his head, thrown to him by the Barmy Army. As he goes to strike a delivery, he mishits and the ball rolls past him – so he quickly turns to swipe it away from the wicket. But as he does so, the handkerchief falls on the ball and stops it rolling. Fielders appeal wildly. What is your decision?

3

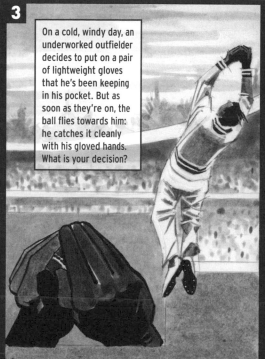

On a cold, windy day, an underworked outfielder decides to put on a pair of lightweight gloves that he's been keeping in his pocket. But as soon as they're on, the ball flies towards him: he catches it cleanly with his gloved hands. What is your decision?

Answers

1) A split ball is not a dead ball – so the striking batsman is out on appeal. For the non-striking batsman to be run out, the ball must have deflected off a member of the fielding side first. If that had happened, both appeals would have been valid but there can be only one dismissal from a ball. In this case the catch would take precedence over the run-out.

2) Not out. There's no law against a player having a knotted hankie on his head and, importantly, the wicket was not broken. At no stage did the batsman do anything illegal.

3) Five penalty runs to the batting side for illegal fielding. The only member of the fielding side who can touch the ball while it is live while wearing gloves is the wicketkeeper. If a fielder deliberately uses a cap or his clothing to intercept the ball, that is illegal fielding and five penalty runs will be awarded to the batting side. John Holder: This happened in a match I umpired in Australia a few years ago, when a fielder, going to stop the ball, found his cap falling off. He took the cap off and stopped the ball with the hand that held the cap. I awarded five penalty runs to the batting side.

Fred Trueman

Full name: Frederick Sewards Trueman
Date of birth: February 6, 1931
Major teams: England, Yorkshire

Tests: 67
Ave: 13.81
Wickets: 307
Bowling ave: 21.57
BBI: 8-31
BBM: 12-119

'Fiery Fred' Trueman was a contender for the title of England's greatest ever fast bowler. Possessing a classical action, fearsome pace, and the will and character to intimidate, he was the first bowler in history to pass the mark of 300 Test wickets. He made his debut in 1952 against India, taking seven wickets, although he had to wait until 1963 to record his best moment – 12 for 119 taken against West Indies.

A volatile figure, Trueman clashed regularly with the cricketing establishment, stopping him from featuring in as many Tests as he should have. But he later put all that bluntness and sharpness of wit to fine use in his role as a commentator and television personality. He died in 2006.

2

A fielder is chasing a ball to the boundary. As he slides to stop it he moves the boundary rope backwards while not in contact with the ball. Then, while not in contact with the boundary, he stops the ball. But if he hadn't moved the boundary rope back the ball would have struck it. Is it a four?

3

A batsman leans over a ball as it pitches, trying to smother the spin. The ball ricochets down off the bat's face, bounces up off the ground, skims the bat's edge and loops to a fielder who catches it. What do you give?

Answers

1) As soon as you notice that a new ball is being used, you must immediately call and signal dead ball. No runs can be scored nor wickets taken. You must also report the incident to the management. John Holder: This situation really shouldn't arise. Before the match both umpires should be au fait with the regulations and the match ball should be handed to the umpires before play starts and when the second innings begins. It should also be the umpire who takes the same match ball on to the field and hands it to the fielding side.

2) No, because the moving of the boundary rope was purely accidental.

3) Not out. To be out for hitting the ball twice it must be intentional and this was not: the ball clearly bounced from the ground to strike the bat. Equally a batsman can only be given out caught from the first strike – in this situation the ball was played into the ground before the catch was taken.

1

A team skittled quickly in a rain-affected match have to follow on. The fielding captain is very keen to have play restarted, as time is short, but the batting captain wants the heavy roller applied to the pitch. What do you do?

2

A big hit sends the ball flying into the crowd: the spectators try but fail to catch the ball, and eventually, after a scramble, you see it returned to the nearest fielder. However, after a further three balls have been bowled and two runs scored you discover that it wasn't the original match ball that was thrown back. What do you do?

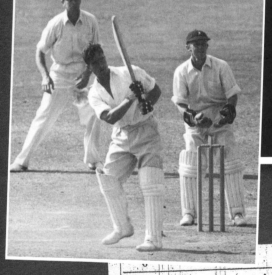

Answers

1) When an innings ends, there must be a minimum interval of 10 minutes before play restarts. During that time the batting captain is allowed to have the pitch rolled for a maximum of seven minutes – so, in this case, he would be allowed to employ the heavy roller for that time.

2) In this situation the match would continue and any runs or wickets taken with the wrong ball would stand. It should be avoided, however, as it is the umpire's responsibility to inspect the ball when it is returned to make sure it is the correct one. Having discovered it you would replace the spectator's ball with one of the spare match balls.

3) You would award the four runs to the batsman. Because the bat slipped out of his hands at the moment of contact when the runs stand. Had he thrown the bat at the ball, either umpire would call and signal 'dead ball' and the runs would not count. If you judge the bat left his hands accidentally you would take no action; however, if you deem that it was thrown at the ball the batsman would also be warned for dangerous and unfair play.

THE MANCHESTER GUARDIAN SATURD

Cricket

PAKISTAN'S ATTACK MASSACRED

Compton and Graveney Merciless

FROM DENYS ROWBOTHAM

TRENT BRIDGE, FRIDAY.

There has been such sad massacre in the second Test match here to-day that were it not for the finest innings one has seen Graveney play and the 278 of Compton, much of which was near to his old inimitable best, one would rather not have to report it. Sheppard declared England's first innings closed at 5.20 p.m., when the score was 558 for six wickets and England led by 401. At the close, more happily, Pakistan, on a still perfect wicket, had made 59 without loss. But their task seems still insuperable.

To-day England scored 437 in just over four and three-quarter hours. It was composed of 84 in 50 minutes by Compton and Simpson this morning, in the course of compiling which Simpson spent 45 minutes in the awful 90s, reached his century with a lovely off-drive, and, then was bowled through making a wretched lined sweep to the next good length ball; a stand of 154 in 90 minutes by Compton and Graveney, of which the latter made 84 before being tempted to drive a richly flighted slower ball of too good length from Kardar; a stand of 192 by Compton and Bailey before the tired hero at last was bowled as he tried to chop a straight good length ball; and 27 further runs from Bailey, Evans, and Wardle.

The Two Principal Efforts

Of the 429 runs scored during the 4¾ hours he was at the wicket Compton made

replacing him himself. The new ball could have been taken some 20 minutes before Kardar began to bowl. He did not take it until after lunch.

Ghazali, a by no means erratic spinner, Kardar did not bowl at all, as he did not try Mohammad Aslam, a googly bowler. Khalid he did not bowl between lunch and tea and only at four o'clock, when the score was 475, did he try Maqsood, a recognised medium-paced change bowler. The analysis shows the burden carried by Khan and Fazal. It was as if the match had quite got out of Kardar's control and he had forgotten what resources he had. The rate of scoring shows how hopelessly tangled his field-placings became and batsmen were helped by repeated mis-fieldings. Compton also was missed crucially at the wicket when only 20 and again in the deep or half deep at 120, 170, and 236.

A Gleam of Hope

At the last, however, there was hope for the morrow. Hanif, as it moved to creative temper by the case of England's subjugation of his own side's poor bowlers, attacked Statham and Bedser at once, hooking and sweeping the former every time he pitched short and driving and cutting the latter. His bat carved his shots to such purpose that in 35 minutes Pakistan's score was 51, of which he had made 35. Appleyard restricted the rate of scoring immediately and Bedser steadied himself superbly so that only 8 runs came in the last 25 minutes. But both batsmen looked much surer, sounder in judgment, and more concentrated in attention than they had done in their first innings. To-morrow, at least

D. C. S. Compton in play during his innings of 278 against Pakistan at Trent Bridge yesterday.

Cricket

SPORTING FINISH AT OLD TRAFFORD

Lancashire partially retrieved a disappointing batting performance against Leicestershire at Old Trafford which had cost them first-innings lead, by a commendable, if futile, bid to win

Rowing

RUSSIANS REACH THREE FINALS

From our Special Correspondent

HENLEY-ON-THAMES, FRIDAY.

The Russian crews did well at Henley Royal Regatta to-day and won through to the finals of the three events in which

3

A batsman going for a big hit loses his grip on the bat and it comes out of his hands the moment it hits the ball. The bat falls to the ground and the ball goes for a four. What action do you take?

Denis Compton

Full name: Denis Charles Scott Compton
Date of birth: May 23, 1918
Major teams: England, Middlesex

Tests: 78
Ave: 50.06
Centuries: 17
Fifties: 28
High score: 278
Wickets: 25
Bowling ave: 56.40

Charismatic and blessed with movie-star looks, Denis Compton was a cricketing great and a sporting polymath. A fluent, stylish batsman who helped lift English cricket from the post-war doldrums, he also played football for Arsenal, winning the FA Cup. But it's as a cricketer – an attacking, risk-taking batsman and an occasional but effective chinaman bowler – that he's principally remembered.

He made his England debut in 1937 against New Zealand and was an immediate success. His career, though, was interrupted by the Second World War (during which he played 12 wartime internationals for the England football team). Post-war, Compton hit his greatest form, when, in 1947, he enjoyed a season no one has matched, scoring 18 centuries and hitting 3,816 runs – both records for any season. However in the final match of the season at Lord's he injured his knee and, though he played on for another decade, he never quite recaptured such form. In 1953, though, he scored the winning runs when England regained the Ashes they had lost in 1936-37. Considered one of England's greatest batsmen – both for the runs and the manner in which he scored them – Compton was also a national celebrity, with his endorsement of Brylcreem one of the first big commercial deals in sport. He died in 1997.

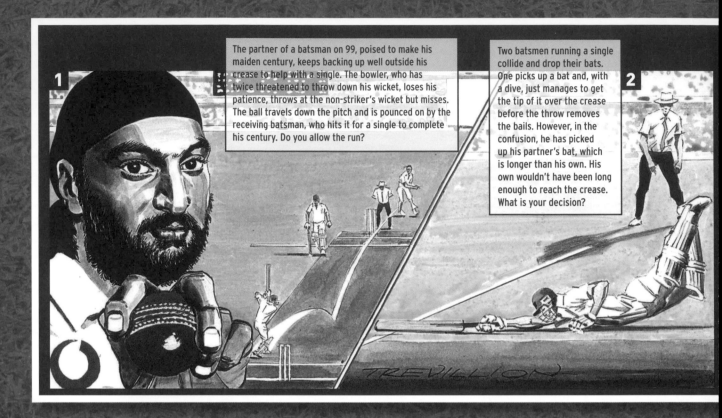

1
The partner of a batsman on 99, poised to make his maiden century, keeps backing up well outside his crease to help with a single. The bowler, who has twice threatened to throw down his wicket, loses his patience, throws at the non-striker's wicket but misses. The ball travels down the pitch and is pounced on by the receiving batsman, who hits it for a single to complete his century. Do you allow the run?

2
Two batsmen running a single collide and drop their bats. One picks up a bat and, with a dive, just manages to get the tip of it over the crease before the throw removes the bails. However, in the confusion, he has picked up his partner's bat, which is longer than his own. His own wouldn't have been long enough to reach the crease. What is your decision?

1
A slow bowler who has bowled three balls over the wicket with his left hand informs you he'll change to bowling around the wicket. You alert the batsman. The bowler then delivers the next ball with his right hand, bowling the surprised batsman. The batsman insists he's not out and that he should have been informed. What is your decision?

2
A slow bowler deceives the batsman, who has advanced down the pitch. The wicketkeeper moves forward to stump him, stumbles and falls on the wicket. He doesn't disturb the bails and the ball hits the wicket. The batsman insists he's not out because the keeper had encroached on the wicket before the ball removed the bails. What is your decision?

KEY MOMENT   Monty Panesar

England v New Zealand
Second Test, Old Trafford,
23-26 May 2008
First innings: 1-101 Second innings: 6-37
England won by six wickets

In the prelude to this Test, much was made of Monty's perceived inferiority to New Zealand's left-arm finger spinner, Daniel Vettori. Vettori was seen to have more experience, more variation and – that attribute so beloved in spinners – more guile. The New Zealand captain had underlined his own merits by taking five wickets for 56 in England's first innings, needling his opponents with a fine display of composed bowling, and placing the Black Caps in a hugely dominant position. Panesar, in contrast, had struggled in the first innings, taking just 1 for 101. However, in his second attempt he soon proved that his less romantic approach to spin bowling – using bounce, frequent if unremarkable spin, and considerable accuracy – could prove equally effective. He took six wickets, including that of Ross Taylor, his 100th wicket in just his 28th Test.

Monty had turned the course of the match in just two-and-a-half hours, as he spun England from the verge of an embarrassing defeat to a fine victory. His six wickets for 37 runs was the spinner's best Test return and proved, again, that he could be England's matchwinner. England were left needing 294 to win, a target they knocked off with an un-English lack of fuss to record the highest successful run-chase at Old Trafford.

Full biography, page 16.

3

An incoming batsman has repaired his favourite bat with three wraps of tape around a crack. The wicketkeeper insists it is illegal, but the batsman says it's standard practice to tape up a cracked bat. What do you decide?

Answers

1) No. The bowler is entitled to try to run the non-striker out, but must do so before he enters his delivery stride. If he misses the stumps, you must immediately call and signal 'dead ball', so that no further action can take place. The striker doesn't get a chance to score runs.

2) Not out. There's no requirement that the batsman must use his own bat. There's a legal restriction on the size of bats, though, which must be no longer than 38 inches and 4.25 inches wide, with the blade made solely of wood. There's no weight restriction.

3) You make the decisions, not the wicketkeeper. A batsman is entitled to use tape on his bat to repair or strengthen it so long as the tape doesn't cause unacceptable damage to the ball. The taping must also not increase the width of the bat by more than 1/16th of an inch.

KEY MOMENT

Shane Warne

England v Australia
First Ashes Test, Old Trafford, 3-7 June 1993
Ball of the Century

In his debut Test against India in 1992, Warne returned figures of one for 128 and there was no real indication of the bowler he would later become. It wasn't until 1993, with a delivery that would later be voted Ball of the Century, that Warne truly arrived, but he did so resoundingly with his first Test delivery in England. After walking in, Warne sent down a leg break to Mike Gatting, a right-handed batsman. The ball headed straight down the pitch before drifting to leg, first gently and then viciously. On bouncing, it gripped and span a monumental 18 inches to the left, clipping the off stump and dismissing a shell-shocked Gatting.

From there Warne's legend quickly grew, and he continued to be a particular scourge to the English. In 1994 he took the first Ashes hat-trick for 91 years and in all he took 172 English wickets, the most Ashes wickets ever, at an average of 22.30.

Full biography, page 10. Foreword, pages 6-7.

3

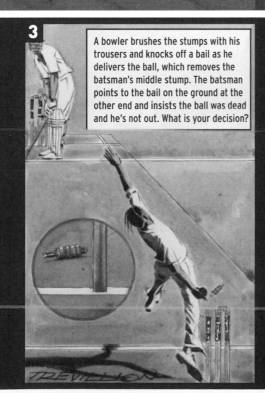

A bowler brushes the stumps with his trousers and knocks off a bail as he delivers the ball, which removes the batsman's middle stump. The batsman points to the bail on the ground at the other end and insists the ball was dead and he's not out. What is your decision?

Answers

1) Not out. The bowler cannot change his mode of delivery, from left arm to right arm or over the wicket to round the wicket, without informing the bowler's end umpire, who will then tell the striker. If the bowler transgresses, as in this case, you will call no ball.

2) You would give the batsman out, bowled, on appeal, as long as the striker's end umpire is convinced the keeper's falling forward on to the wicket was purely accidental.

3) The bowler breaking the wicket at his end in delivery does not cause the ball to become dead. It's still live and on appeal you would give the batsman out.

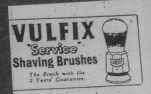

LAKER BEATS AUSTRALIA

The 19-Wicket Masterpiece

England 459; Australia 84 and 205

By Denys Rowbotham

A superb piece of bowling by J. C. Laker not only brought England victory by an innings and 170 runs in the fourth Test match at Old Trafford yesterday (and continued custody of the "Ashes") but created several remarkable records at the same time.

First, by taking Australia's eight remaining wickets Laker became the first bowler ever to take all ten in one innings in a Test match. These ten wickets, added to his nine in the first innings, also gave him more wickets in a single Test match than any other bowler has obtained in cricket's history. Seventeen of his nineteen wickets were taken in succession, which may also be a record. His aggregate of 51 wickets from five matches against the Australians this season seems unlikely also ever to have been beaten.

Significant records rarely are broken unless the performance is worthy. But a record which derives from an aggregate may be achieved luckily, with the willing connivance of a partner, or with a performance at the crucial moment below the record-breaker's best. More than once, one suspects, ten wickets in an innings have been taken because the bowler at the other end has "soft-pedalled" for the last few overs or minutes. Yesterday, however, Laker's records were achieved in the highest tradition. To the end of the day at half-past five Lock used every stratagem to take even one wicket which would have quickened England's victory. Field placings, even after the ninth wicket had fallen, were adjusted subtly to enable him to take it had Johnson made only a single error. So that when Laker finally had Maddocks leg-before and the crowd burst into rounds and rounds of cheering he knew that the proudest distinctions had never been gained more genuinely.

Not a Sticky Wicket

Laker's performance becomes still more outstanding when it is emphasised, as it must be, that yesterday's wicket was never strictly sticky. Until about a quarter of an hour before lunch the ball turned slightly but exasperatingly slowly and never with a hint of bite or nip. Then the wicket still was a mud patch. Within 45 minutes of the start at 11.40 in fact Laker was replaced by Oakman, and fifteen minutes later Lock gave way to Statham. The soft surface helped an accurate Statham no more than it had Laker and Lock. Craig and McDonald had only to keep their heads, make no palpable misjudgment, and sustain a watchful concentration to survive without hint of obvious difficulty. They were able as well to cut and hook anything short with impunity.

All the time a strong wind was drying a wet wicket as amiably as one can well be dried. At 1.10, however, when Laker replaced Bailey at the City end, the sun came out and shone brightly, if not hotly, until roughly an hour after lunch. Within ten minutes Laker had made a ball pop, and before lunch he was turning the ball markedly more sharply and quickly. Clearly after lunch it would soon be obvious whether Australia was to save or lose the match.

The answer came more quickly than one had expected. May promptly changed Lock to the city and Laker to the more dangerous Stretford end. Twice in Laker's first over McDonald was in trouble; twice in Lock's first over balls jumped nastily. And fifteen minutes after lunch Craig was out. Laker made an off-break turn sharply from a full-length richly flighted; Craig played a half-cock, missed, and was leg-before. Ten minutes later Mackay pushed forward to flighted spin he did not smother and Oakman took the catch

[Continued on page 4

A bowler delivers a no ball . . .

. . . which beats the bat. The ball hits the striker's thigh pad . . .

Answer

First you would signal no ball, then the signal for a leg bye and then for four runs. The leg bye signal is specifically to inform the scorers that the runs are not credited to the striker. Each signal must be individually acknowledged by the scorers and you should never restart play until all your signals have been acknowledged.

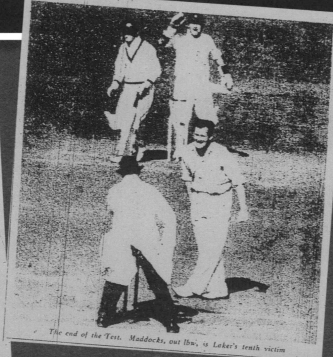

The end of the Test. Maddocks, out lbw, is Laker's tenth victim

... and flies away over the boundary. What is the sequence of signals you give?

TREVILLION.

Jim Laker

Full name: James Charles Laker
Date of birth: February 9, 1922
Major teams: England, Essex, Surrey

Tests: 46
Ave: 14.08
Fifties: 2
High score: 63
Wickets: 193
Bowling ave: 21.24
BBI: 10-53 **BBM:** 19-90

Jim Laker is one of the few cricketers to have the honour of a Test match informally named after him. 'Laker's Test', England against Australia at Old Trafford in 1956, was the stage for one of the most famous and extraordinary individual performances ever: Laker destroyed the Australian line-up, taking 19 wickets for 90 in the match, including 10 for 53 in the second innings. This is both a Test and first-class record and is likely to stay so.

An off-spin bowler, Laker was one of England's greatest proponents of spin bowling. Always accurate, he became lethal if – as at Old Trafford in '56 – the pitch was taking spin. He formed a famous partnership with another great English spin-bowler, the left-arm orthodox Tony Lock, with whom he also combined for Surrey. While his overall achievements are often overshadowed by one incredible Test, the tailend of his career was initially marred by one bold decision: the publication of an autobiography that was scathing about Peter May, his Surrey and England captain. Laker died in 1986.

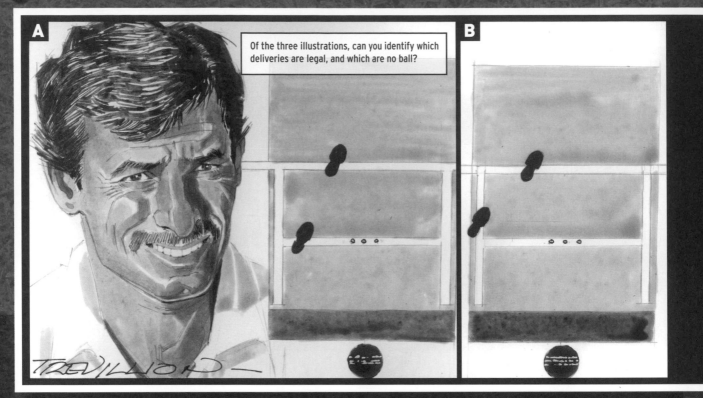

Of the three illustrations, can you identify which deliveries are legal, and which are no ball?

Richard Hadlee

Full name: Sir Richard John Hadlee
Date of birth: July 3, 1951
Major teams: New Zealand, Canterbury, Nottinghamshire, Tasmania

Tests: 86	Wickets: 431	Fifties: 4
Ave: 27.16	Bowling ave: 22.29	High score: 79
Centuries: 2	BBI: 9-52 BBM: 15-123	Wickets: 158
Fifties: 15	ODIs: 115	Bowling ave: 21.56
High score: 151*	Ave: 21.61	BBM: 5-25

A member of a cricketing dynasty – his father, ex-wife and two of his brothers all played international cricket – Richard Hadlee came to represent the coming of age of New Zealand cricket. His country's first truly great international, he was both a world-class fast bowler and a heroic all-rounder.

His bowling ranked alongside the very best. Starting with an obsession with out-and-out pace, he gradually shifted the emphasis to guile and accuracy. He had the ability to encourage bounce and movement from any pitch. His bowling inspired some of the most significant feats in New Zealand's cricketing history, including when, in 1978, his 10 wickets helped his team to their first ever win over England. He was the first bowler to pass the 400 Test wickets mark, and he retired with a then-world record 431 Test victims.

1

The ball passes very close to the stumps at the same time as a strong gust of wind, and one of the bails flies off. The fielding side appeal, but the batsman claims it was the wind, not the ball, that removed the bail. What is your decision?

2

A player has been off the field with a pulled muscle for an hour. As soon as he returns, he's brought on to bowl. A batsman complains, insisting the laws state that the length of time a player spends off the field injured is the same length of time he must wait once he returns to play before being allowed to bowl. Is he right?

Answers

1) Not out. The benefit of the doubt in this situation goes to the batsman, and you can only give him out if you're absolutely sure that some part of his person or bat or the ball itself broke the wicket.

2) At first-class and international level, the batsman is correct: he's not out – the bouncer limit has been exceeded and you should award another no ball, John Holder: I was the umpire in a similar situation in a county match some years ago at Lord's between Middlesex and Durham. Phil Tufnell came in at number 11, facing Durham's fast-medium bowler Marc Symington. Knowing that Tuffers didn't relish fast bowling, Symington immediately bowled two bouncers. I told him he'd reached his limit for the over. He then bowled another bouncer which I no-balled. Then he did it again – so I no-balled it and gave him a final warning for dangerous and unfair bowling. If he'd done it again after that, he would have been banned from bowling for the rest of the innings.

3) The batsman is right. The umpires will have made a note of the time the fielder went off. On his return they'll confer to determine how long he was off the field. First-class and international regulations state that he cannot bowl until he has spent as much time on the pitch as he was off it.

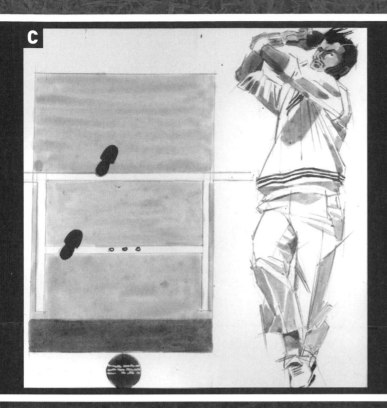

C

Answers

1) Legal, because part of the front foot is behind the popping crease.

2) No ball, because though part of the front foot is behind the popping crease, his back foot, if grounded, is cutting the return crease.

3) No ball, because no part of the front foot is behind the popping crease. It's important to remember, with regards to no balls caused by foot faults, that the edge of the crease marking nearest the wicket is the actual crease, irrespective of how wide the painted line is.

John Holder: In my 26 years umpiring, Sir Richard Hadlee was by far the most single-minded, totally focused bowler I ever saw. When he came out to bowl, his sole objective was getting wickets. He would go to the bowling crease, measure five boot lengths, make a line behind the wicket with the tip of his boot and then ask the umpire to stand there. He was so meticulous about his bowling run-up that he knew exactly where he wanted the umpire, within inches, to stand.

After bowling the first ball he would say, as he walked past the umpire: 'If I get close to no-balling on the front foot or running on the pitch, please tell me.' Such was his desire to take wickets, he didn't wish to miss the chance of getting a wicket by bowling a no ball. Nor did he want his rhythm to be broken by repeated warnings.

It was fascinating standing at the bowler's end watching Hadlee pressurise batsman after batsman with relentless accuracy mixed with subtle variations of pace, swing, seam and bounce.

From the moment he walked into the ground, arrived in the dressing room and opened his 'cricket coffin' to take out his gear, Hadlee was the ultimate professional. Taped inside the 'coffin' lid was an A4 sheet of paper with a check-list of his bowling drills. He'd refer to this sheet before and after each interval and, if he wasn't satisfied with his bowling, he could spend almost the entire interval rechecking his list. Sir Richard Hadlee stands alongside the greats of the game.

KEY MOMENT

Paul Collingwood

Australia v England
Second Ashes Test, Adelaide,
1-5 December 2006.
First innings: 206 runs, 515 mins, 392 balls, 16 fours. Second innings: 22*, 198 mins, 119 balls, 2 fours. Australia won by 6 wickets.

On the fourth day of the first Test of the 2006-07 Ashes, Paul Collingwood was stumped on 96, skipping down the pitch to Shane Warne. It precipitated a typical English collapse, as they threw away what appeared a certain draw. However, in the next Test in Adelaide, he hit a fantastic 206. For lengthy periods of the first day Collingwood scored slowly, tied down by the accuracy of Warne. But once he was joined by Kevin Pietersen – who went on to score 158 and with whom Collingwood put on 310 for the fourth wicket – the run-rate picked up and by stumps Collingwood was 98 not out. He passed 100, his third century, in the second over of the second day and eventually brought up his double century with a lofted shot off spinner Michael Clarke. Collingwood was finally dismissed, caught by Adam Gilchrist off the bowling of Stuart Clark, after 515 minutes. It was a magnificent innings, featuring Collingwood's trademark mixture of nudges and nurdles, and should have set up a famous win for England. Instead they succumbed to one of their most devastating defeats, losing by six wickets.

Collingwood's 206 was the first double century scored by an Englishman in Australia since Wally Hammond 70 years earlier, and with it he became only the eighth English player to score a double in the Ashes. Unfortunately for him, it was also the seventh highest score ever made in a losing cause.

Full biography, page 18.

3

A bowler delivers a bouncer, but you call it wide. He then does it again – another wide. His third delivery is yet another bouncer, but this time it's on line: the batsman swipes, and is caught off his glove. But the batsman insists he's not out because the bowler exceeded the number of bouncers he can bowl in an over. The bowler, though, insists the first two, being wides, did not count. What do you do?

Peter May

Full name: Peter Barker Howard May
Date of birth: December 31, 1929
Major teams: England, Surrey

Tests: 66	Fifties: 22
Ave: 46.77	Centuries: 13
	High score: 285*

Cricket came naturally to PBH May. At the age of 14 he scored a century for Charterhouse against Harrow, and it was quickly obvious that he was destined for great things. In 1951 he was selected for England – against South Africa at Headingley – at the age of 21 and scored a magnificent 138. He became an integral part of both the all-conquering Surrey side of the 50s and of the England team that never dropped a series between 1952 and 1958.

A classical batsman, both instinctive and considered, there was something heroic about May: he was tall, handsome and quintessentially English. He won the captaincy in 1956 and proved to be an inspirational and authoritative leader: only Michael Vaughan has won more than May's 20 Tests as captain. The responsibility also seemed to improve his batting: in 1957 he shared a stand of 411 with Colin Cowdrey, England's record partnership for any wicket. By the late 50s, however, illness and an apparent loss of passion for the game made his appearances more infrequent; he retired from first-class cricket in 1963. In the 1980s he suffered a largely dismal time as England's chairman of selectors, and died in 1994.

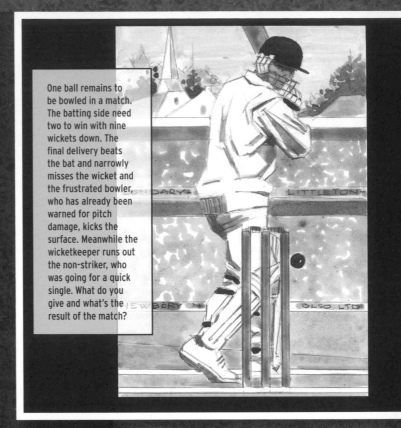

One ball remains to be bowled in a match. The batting side need two to win with nine wickets down. The final delivery beats the bat and narrowly misses the wicket and the frustrated bowler, who has already been warned for pitch damage, kicks the surface. Meanwhile the wicketkeeper runs out the non-striker, who was going for a quick single. What do you give and what's the result of the match?

Sachin Tendulkar

Full name: Sachin Ramesh Tendulkar
Date of birth: April 24, 1973
Major teams: India, Mumbai, Yorkshire

Tests: 154	ODIs: 419
Ave: 54.30	Ave: 44.26
Centuries: 40	Centuries: 42
Fifties: 51	Fifties: 90
High score: 248*	High score: 186*
Wickets: 42	Wickets: 154
Bowling av: 53.02	Bowling av: 44.12
BBI: 3-10	BBM: 5-32
BBM: 3-14	

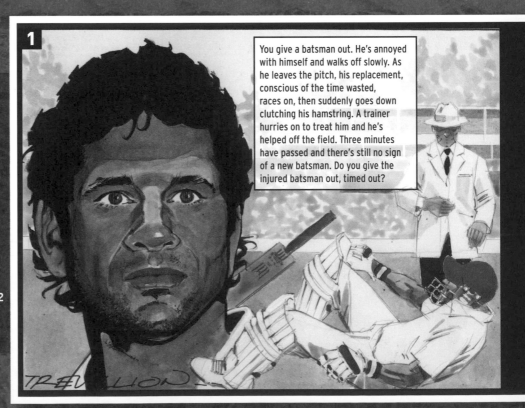

1

You give a batsman out. He's annoyed with himself and walks off slowly. As he leaves the pitch, his replacement, conscious of the time wasted, races on, then suddenly goes down clutching his hamstring. A trainer hurries on to treat him and he's helped off the field. Three minutes have passed and there's still no sign of a new batsman. Do you give the injured batsman out, timed out?

Sachin Tendulkar – 'The Little Master' – is among the finest batsman ever known and the greatest of his generation. Many of his stats in both forms of the game are unrivalled: he has scored a record number of runs in Test and one-day internationals and an unprecedented 40 Test and 42 ODI centuries. For a player so successful, and so elegant, he has a surprisingly unorthodox technique, leading with a heavy bottom hand.

His brilliance was obvious from the start: he scored his maiden hundred on his first-class debut, aged just 15 years and 232 days. His Test debut came at 16 and he made his first Test century – against England at Old Trafford – at 17. His method of run scoring became gradually more staid as his career progressed, but he retained his fluency.

In India Tendulkar is more than a cricketing hero, he's a cultural icon, making him one of the most famous sportsmen in the world and the wealthiest cricketer of all time.

2

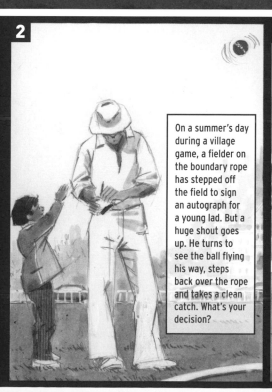

On a summer's day during a village game, a fielder on the boundary rope has stepped off the field to sign an autograph for a young lad. But a huge shout goes up. He turns to see the ball flying his way, steps back over the rope and takes a clean catch. What's your decision?

3

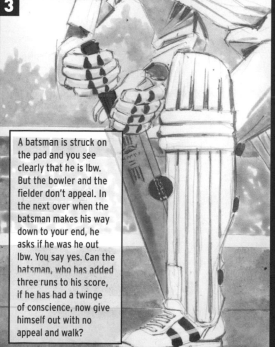

A batsman is struck on the pad and you see clearly that he is lbw. But the bowler and the fielder don't appeal. In the next over when the batsman makes his way down to your end, he asks if he was he out lbw. You say yes. Can the batsman, who has added three runs to his score, if he has had a twinge of conscience, now give himself out with no appeal and walk?

91

Brett Lee

Full name: Brett Lee
Date of birth: November 8, 1976
Major teams: Australia, New South Wales

Tests: 74	ODIs: 173
Ave: 20.41	Ave: 17.44
Fifties: 5	Fifties: 2
High score: 64	High score: 57
Wickets: 309	Wickets: 303
Bowling ave: 30.11	Bowling ave: 22.95
BBI: 5-30	BBM: 5-22
BBM: 9-171	

For a long time Brett Lee was considered Australia's luxury bowler: capable of bowling at well over 90mph, he was as fast as any in the world, but could prove erratic. Injuries and the unparalleled strength of Australia's bowling line-up ensured that he was initially limited to bit parts and ODIs. However, he was one of only a few Australians to enhance his reputation in the 2005 Ashes series, during which he excelled with both bat and ball, and since then has become a mainstay of the line-up. The retirements of other senior bowlers have given him additional responsibility and he now leads the attack.

The added responsibility also brought maturity. Whereas once he focused on pure speed and relied heavily on bouncers and yorkers, Lee latterly added accuracy and greater variation. These improvements have helped take him to fourth in Australia's all-time Test wickets takers, with 309 victims. He has also proved a hugely successful ODI bowler, taking 303 wickets at an average of 22.95. A charismatic and youthful figure, Lee says he'll try to launch an acting career when he retires from cricket.

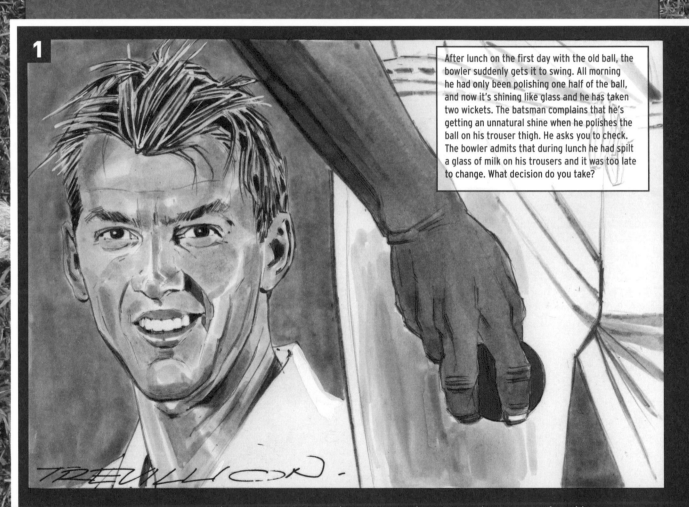

1

After lunch on the first day with the old ball, the bowler suddenly gets it to swing. All morning he had only been polishing one half of the ball, and now it's shining like glass and he has taken two wickets. The batsman complains that he's getting an unnatural shine when he polishes the ball on his trouser thigh. He asks you to check. The bowler admits that during lunch he had spilt a glass of milk on his trousers and it was too late to change. What decision do you take?

Answers

1. The law is clear that no artificial substances can be used to polish the ball and the bowler has admitted that he has done so. Artificially changing the condition of the ball – ball tampering – is a serious offence. In this case, you should change the ball for one of similar wear to the old ball before it was tampered with. You should also notify both batsmen of the change, award five penalty runs to the batting side and explain your decision to the fielding captain. You should also notify the captain of the batting side and report the matter to the fielding team's management and the governing body.

2. Anybody delivering a ball three feet beyond the popping crease and bowling a bouncer at a batsman has done so deliberately. You should call no ball immediately and give the bowler a warning for dangerous and unfair bowling. The fact that he has been repeatedly hit to the boundary immediately before the overstepping will be a factor, and to overstep by that distance isn't accidental.

John Holder: Many years ago I had a similar experience in a county match between Derbyshire and Gloucestershire at Derby. In the home team's

2

A fast bowler has been slammed for three successive sixes. His next delivery is a wild bouncer. He had overstepped the popping crease by a yard and the batsman, still dazed from the ball that cannoned into his helmet, leaves the field. Would you have a word with the bowler immediately or would you wait to see if he repeats what borders on an illegal 'no ball'? And if he did repeat the yard over the popping crease gamesmanship, what action would you take?

3

A slow bowler is bowling wearing two different coloured shoes – a red and a blue. The batsman complains that, when the bowler dances up to the wicket, it knocks his concentration. Would you insist that the bowler wears matching white boots?

second innings, Courtney Walsh opened the bowling at my end to Kim Barnett and Peter Bowler. Walsh bowled very fast but constantly overstepped the popping crease and I no-balled him. To add to his woes, the batsmen were scoring at a fast rate. Walsh told me he wanted to bowl around the wicket so I told Barnett and asked if he wanted the sight screen moved and he said yes. This seemed to annoy the bowler.

Barnett played the next ball defensively for no run and as Walsh walked by me to his mark he told Peter Bowler, the non-striker, to 'wipe the f***ing smile off his face'. I immediately reprimanded him for obscene language. Barnett got a single off the next ball, bringing Bowler to the striker's end. There was no doubt that this act was deliberate. I called and signalled no ball and informed the bowler, his captain, my colleague and the batsmen that this was a warning for, what was called at the time, intimidatory bowling. Walsh was also reported to the board and received a caution.

Walsh came back over the wicket, ran up and hurled a head-high beamer from 18 inches over the popping crease directly at Bowler's head. Luckily the ball missed, but it landed awkwardly in front of Jack Russell, nearly taking his head off as it flashed by to the boundary.

3. There's no law against a player wearing differently coloured shoes. If the batsman is looking at the bowler's shoes he has a big problem, as he should instead be looking at the ball in the bowler's hand. He will have an idea of which direction the bowler is trying to bowl the ball by the way he grips it.

Matt Prior

Full name:
Matthew James Prior
Date of birth:
February 26, 1982
Major teams:
England, Sussex

Tests: 10
Ct: 28 St: 0
Ave: 40.14
Centuries: 1
Fifties: 4
High score: 126*

ODIs: 33
Ct: 39 St: 3
Centuries: 0
Fifties: 1
High score: 52

1

A bowler, who was repeatedly no-balled before lunch, asks you to keep an eye on his run-up and warn him when he looks to be close to over-stepping. The batsman overhears and insists your duty is to umpire, not to act as a bowling coach. What is your reply?

2
Two fielders chase the ball to the boundary. A yard from the boundary rope the first fielder to the ball slips but manages to divert the ball back to the second fielder, without touching the line. The second fielder scoops up the ball but slides into the first fielder who is half over the line. He takes the ball while in contact with the original fielder, gets to his feet and throws the ball in. The batsmen have already taken three runs – but should a boundary be awarded?

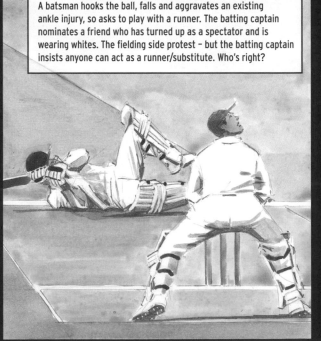

Matt Prior had a dream England Test debut, scoring a ferocious 126 not out against West Indies at Lord's in 2007. English cricket writers proclaimed the end of the wicketkeeper problem, which had been raging since the retirement of Alec Stewart. But, although he scored four half centuries and kept his average above 40, he failed to sustain his initial form with the bat, his offensive stoke play proving less effective against stronger bowling attacks. However, it was his keeping that really undermined him. Poor series against India and Sri Lanka, in which handling mistakes and drops were rife, ensured that he was no longer the best option as wicketkeeper and he was dropped for the tour to New Zealand. A perceived cockiness and an excessive vocality didn't help his cause.

He returned in August 2008 for the 4-0 ODI series victory over South Africa. Opening the batting, Prior failed to pass 50 but averaged over 40 individually and 87 as a partnership with Ian Bell. His rehabilitation was complete – he had played his way back into contention for a Test spot.

1

A match is scheduled for four days, but no play takes place on days one or two due to rain. No play is possible until after lunch on day three. If the batting side want to enforce the follow-on, what is the minimum lead they need?

2
A batsman hooks the ball, falls and aggravates an existing ankle injury, so asks to play with a runner. The batting captain nominates a friend who has turned up as a spectator and is wearing whites. The fielding side protest – but the batting captain insists anyone can act as a runner/substitute. Who's right?

3

A misfield prompts the batsmen to go for a second run but in their haste one drops his bat. When the ball is thrown in, with both batsmen safely home, the bowler fields the ball with the dropped bat, knocking it up into the air and allowing it to bounce three times on the blade before handing the bat back. Everyone in the ground laughs and applauds – what do you do?

Answers

1) Inform the batsman that the umpire is entirely within his rights to warn a player who is on the verge of infringing the law – county cricket umpires regularly warn bowlers when they're close to no-balling.

2) The law doesn't specifically cover this but in this instance the MCC have given a ruling that a boundary four should be awarded, because the second fielder, although legally in play, is in contact with an object – his team-mate, who is lying on, and across, the boundary rope.

3) If, in your opinion, the ball is still live this would count as illegal fielding and you'd award five penalty runs to the batting side. John Holder: Many years ago at a county match between Essex and Nottinghamshire, John Lever of Essex bowled from my end to Clive Rice, the Notts captain. Rice drove the ball and Keith Pont gave chase. As Rice grounded his bat at my end on the first run, it slipped from his hand and he completed two more runs without it. Pont threw in the ball to Lever who picked up the bat and knocked it into the air. I awarded five penalty runs to Notts for illegal fielding as I believed the ball to be live. The bowler wasn't amused.

Keith Miller

Full name: Keith Ross Miller
Date of birth: November 28, 1919
Major teams: Australia, New South Wales, Nottinghamshire, Victoria

Tests: 55
Ave: 36.97
Centuries: 7
Fifties: 13
High score: 147
Wickets: 170
Bowling ave: 22.97
BBI: 7-60 BBM: 10-152

Possibly Australia's greatest all-rounder, Keith 'Nugget' Miller's good looks helped make him a true cricketing celebrity. A classy batsman, with an excellent square drive, he scored 181 in his debut first-class match. Although he started his career principally as a batsman, the Australia team had such strength in batting that the onus was placed on his bowling. A versatile and pacy bowler, he moved in off a short run, but could then deliver any ball. From a part-time bowler he progressed to opening the bowling for his country, forming a famous new-ball partnership with Ray Lindwall.

Miller, who died in 2004, had fought with distinction as a pilot in the Second World War, and this informed his subsequent attitude to life and cricket: carefree and irreverent, he sometimes seemed so aware that there was more to life than cricket that he was unconcerned whether his team won or lost. Don Bradman disapproved of such an approach and, when appointed to the Australian Board, prevented Miller from ever captaining his country. Miller had always struggled with authority: during the war he was disciplined several times for insulting or threatening superior officers. But it endeared him to cricket fans and also helped him keep cricket in perspective.

'Pressure?' he once said. 'I'll tell you what pressure is. Pressure is a Messerschmitt up your arse – playing cricket is not.'

3

It's the final over of a limited-overs game and the batting side need seven to win. On strike is a tailender, off strike is a middle-order batsman. The tailender defends the first ball on to the strip right in front of the bowler. They go for the quick single – and to stop the bowler from picking up the ball to claim a run-out, the non-striking batsman kicks the ball away. The batsman claims it was an accident. What is your decision?

1 A batsman drives the ball back down the pitch and the bowler fields it. In an attempt to run out the striker, the bowler tries to throw the ball at speed to the wicketkeeper, but his aim is off and it flies at the batsman's face. Instinctively, the batsman swats it away with his bat, over the boundary. The bowler insists the batsman hit the ball twice. What do you give?

2 A batsman, attempting a quick single, isn't paying attention and runs straight into the bowler, who hadn't moved aside. They both fall to the ground as the fielder hits the stumps. The batsman claims he was impeded, but the bowler insists the batsman had to avoid him. The fielder says the batsman would have been run out anyway. What is your decision?

TREVILLION

Answers

1) Award four runs. The bowler is wrong; the striker's action is a reflex one in self-defence. Whether the ball had struck him or not, he would be awarded runs for an overthrow, as long as he had struck the ball originally.

2) He's run out on appeal. It is the striker's responsibility to run around the bowler who is in his normal follow-through path. Only if the bowler deliberately impedes him is it obstruction.

3) Award the runs. The striker must remember that whichever guard he has taken when the bowler starts his run, off side and leg side remain thus. If he changes his stance after that, he can be given out lbw if the ball pitches behind his legs, turns back and would have hit the wicket but struck the pads instead.

Ricky Ponting   KEY MOMENT

Australia v India
Melbourne, 26-30 December 2003
First innings: 257 runs, 590 mins, 458 balls, 25 fours.
Second innings: 31* runs, 73 mins, 59 balls, 3 fours.
Australia won by nine wickets.

With this knock of 257, Ponting joined Don Bradman as the only player to have scored three double centuries in a single year. Ponting's other doubles in 2003 were 206 against West Indies and 242 against India in the previous Test at Adelaide. This innings in Melbourne meant that the Australian became only the fifth player to score back-to-back double centuries after Wally Hammond, Bradman, Graeme Smith and Vinod Kambli.

2003 was the year that Ponting proved he had stepped into the highest strata of Test batsmen. On day two, he played an innings of great maturity, displaying both patience and ruthlessness. Having passed 100 – his 20th career century – he survived a catch on 126 but otherwise batted without offering a chance. He was finally dismissed when stumped by Parthiv Patel off leg-spinner Anil Kumble.

It brought his run tally to 1,503 in 2003, the most scored in a year by an Australian and the third highest ever. Even more astounding, though, was his average of 100.20 for the year. Full biography, page 20.

3

A batsman adopts a right-handed stance as the bowler places his fielders. But when the bowler gets into his delivery stride, the batsman changes to a left-handed stance and hits the ball through the unprotected field for four. The bowler insists this was gamesmanship and the runs shouldn't count. What is your decision?

A fast bowler, still nine yards from the crease, suddenly unleashes a fierce ball with a perfect bowling action. The shocked batsman is caught by surprise: the ball beats him and knocks his middle stump clean out of the ground. There's a huge appeal – what is your decision?

TREVILLION

Answers

1) **Give the batsman out.** Once the bowler has started his run-up, the ball is live – the bowler is allowed to deliver it at any time. All you need to be concerned about is that the striker is ready and that the ball isn't delivered outside the return crease.

2) **Not out.** If the bails have been removed from the top of the wicket, the fielder can only get a run-out by taking a stump out of the ground with the same hand that is holding the ball. John Holder: Something like this happened in a televised game at Cardiff, with me at the bowler's end. With both batsmen marooned, the fielder nearest the stumps caught the ball with one hand, then pulled a stump out with the other hand and appealed. Fortunately for him, a nearby team-mate knew the laws a little better – he snatched the ball from his colleague and then correctly removed a stump with both hands while clutching the ball.

3) **Do not intervene** – no law has been broken and the opposing captain has no right to complain. John Holder: No one can prove that having steak or anything else inside the gloves helps with catching. In the 2008 World Cup final in Barbados Sri Lanka complained that Adam Gilchrist had a squash ball inside the batting glove on his left hand, giving him an unfair advantage. Gilchrist's thinking was to relax the grip on the bat to make him play straighter and more effectively. All perfectly legal and hugely successful. The laws deal only with external equipment, so the complaint was rightly dismissed.

KEY MOMENT

Kevin Pietersen

England v West Indies
Headingley, 25-28 May 2007
First innings: 226 runs, 432 mins, 262 balls, 24 fours, 2 sixes.
England won by an innings and 283 runs.

KP had developed the unfortunate habit of getting out for 158, a score for which he had been dismissed three times. He broke this marker with a stylish four off Jerome Taylor and went on to build a ferocious innings of 226. Although his opponents were an admittedly weak West Indian side, it was a monumental, match-winning performance.

For much of his innings Pietersen belied his reputation as a show-pony, displaying a solid, efficient maturity. He retained, however, his ability to destroy an attack, with a parade of fours through the leg side. A two scored with a leg-side push brought up his first double century from just 250 balls. With the personal milestone passed and rain forecast, Pietersen broke lose, hitting his first six of the innings off Chris Gayle's bowling. Eventually he holed out off the bowling of Dwayne Bravo, but by then he had made the highest individual Test score by an Englishman since Graham Gooch's 333 in 1990.

Full biography, page 14.

A bowler takes a hat-trick and then, in the following over, his team mate also does the hat-trick, taking the last three wickets. Both bowlers want the match ball, which you're holding. Who gets it?

TREVILLION

Answers

1) **It is not your decision.** The ball belongs to the home club's authority. Permission must be obtained for the ball to be given away, because it's essential that used balls are kept as spares to be used for other matches in the event of a ball becoming unusable or being lost.

2) **A twelfth man cannot act as a runner.** He can only field. The runner should be someone who has already batted. But if the openers are still together, one of the tailenders will act as a runner. The runner must wear the same external equipment as the striker he is running for, including carrying a bat.

3) **Many players eat bananas or energy-giving snacks during drinks intervals, so there's nothing preventing someone eating a hotdog. However it's important to maintain the image and integrity of the game, so players should be discouraged from eating food during such breaks.** John Holder: Several years ago I umpired a county match with Barrie Meyer at Hove, coming to the end of the season. With Sussex fielding in a game meandering to a tame finish, John Barclay, the home captain, ordered alcoholic drinks onto the field. He and his players sat in the grass in front of the committee room sipping their drinks, in protest at earlier criticism from some committee men. It was quite amusing.

2 With the batsmen going for a risky short run, the wicketkeeper races after the ball, dropping one of his gloves on the ground as he goes. But as the glove drops, it hits the wicket, removing both bails. The wicketkeeper then spins and hurls the ball back to a fielder at the stumps. The batsman is stranded – but with both bails already down, the fielder, holding the ball, decides to kick the stumps over, then appeals. Do you give the batsman out?

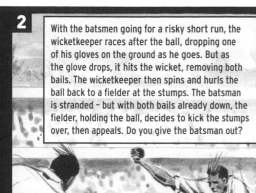

3

Just after tea, you notice, to your surprise, that the wicketkeeper is carefully putting two large fresh steaks in his gloves, and removing two old ones. The opposing captain is outraged, and complains that the steaks are clearly the reason why the wicketkeeper hasn't dropped a ball all day – the meat providing an illegal extra soft cushion in his gloves. What is your response?

Andrew Symonds

Full name: Andrew Symonds
Date of birth: June 9, 1975
Major teams: Australia, Gloucestershire, Kent, Lancashire

Tests: 24	Bowling ave: 36.33	Centuries: 6
Ave: 41.90	BBI: 3-50	Fifties: 29
Centuries: 2	BBM: 5-56	High score: 156
Fifties: 9		Wickets: 129
High score: 162*	ODIs: 193	Bowling ave: 37.68
Wickets: 24	Ave: 40.37	BBM: 5-18

Andrew Symonds is one of the most exciting match winners in world cricket. A talented all-rounder, the Australian can bowl either off-spin or medium pace and is a fine fielder, but it's his batting that has garnered the most attention. A big-hitting, explosive player, he's best known for his ability to hit sixes. Aged just 20, he set world records for the most sixes in an innings (16) and a match (20) when playing for Gloucestershire against Glamorgan.

Symonds struggled on his introduction to international cricket, as his early years in Australia's one-day side were marred by over-ambition and unnecessary dismissals. But the 2003 World Cup proved a turning point, when he struck a masterful 145 against Pakistan. Following that innings he averaged over 40 in ODIs and has taken 129 wickets at a respectable 37.68. His Test career has proved frustrating, though, as he failed to break into a settled side. After several years of being in and out of the team, he again had a career-changing innings: a brutal 156 at the MCG in the 2006-07 Ashes. The only impediment to his progression has been his attitude: he has been in trouble with the Australian Board for getting drunk before a match in 2005 and for going fishing when he should have been present at a team meeting in 2008.

2 A side are batting one short in a second innings due to an injury suffered in their first innings. A few overs later another batsman is hurt, but can carry on with a runner. Can the official twelfth man, who has fielded for their entire innings, be the runner?

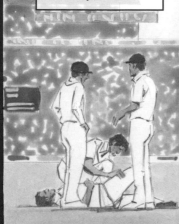

3

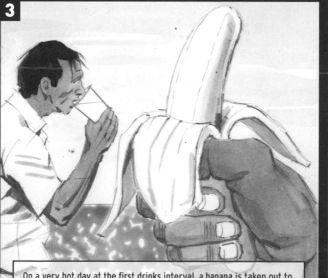

On a very hot day at the first drinks interval, a banana is taken out to one of the home players. The away wicketkeeper notices this and, at the lunchtime interval, asks for a hotdog to be taken out at the next drinks interval. When the interval arrives, the home captain objects to the wicketkeeper eating the hotdog. The wicketkeeper shouts: 'If your player can eat a banana, I can eat a hotdog.' What do you do?

1

The batsman on strike edges the ball through the slips and sets off for a risky run. Desperate to make his ground at the bowler's end, he runs down the middle of the pitch. The ball is thrown towards the bowler's wicket but hits the striker, preventing it from hitting the wicket while he's out of his ground. The wicketkeeper appeals for obstruction. What is your decision?

2

The captains walk out and exchange teams but, just before the toss is about to take place the skies open and you immediately leave the field. A whole day is lost and the next day, in different conditions, one of the captains wants a change of player. Can he do so?

Answers

1) Out, for obstruction. To be given out for obstruction it has to be seen as deliberate by the umpire. In this case the fact that the striker has run down the middle of the pitch, when he knows he is supposed to run along the sides to reduce damaging it, means you must view it as deliberate.

2) No. Once teams have been nominated there cannot be changes without the consent of the opposing captain.

3) You refuse the appeal because if they fall back into the groove it is not out. Despite the balls fusing together the appeal is still rejected. However, you would replace the balls with fresh ones if available or, if none are available, continue the match without balls at both ends.

Andrew Flintoff

KEY MOMENT

England v Australia
Second Ashes Test,
Edgbaston, 4-7 August 2005
First innings: 68 runs, 74 mins, 62 balls, 6 fours, 5 sixes & 3-52.

Second innings: 73 runs, 133 mins, 86 balls, 6 fours, 4 sixes & 4-79.
England won by 2 runs

It had been 18 years since England had last won the Ashes, and a heavy defeat in the first Test of the 2005 series had undermined England's hopes of ending that run. However, after Aussie captain Ricky Ponting made the inexplicable decision to insert England at Edgbaston, the hosts came out fighting, scoring 407 runs in a single day, with Freddie bludgeoning a fierce 68 from just 62 balls, including five sixes. In his second innings he was equally explosive, scoring 73.

With the ball he took three for 52 and four for 79, but it was one spell in particular that is best remembered. Australia were 47 for no wicket in their second innings when Flintoff was thrown the ball. Though he missed out on a hat-trick carried over from the first innings, he dismissed Justin Langer for his third wicket in four deliveries and brought Ponting to the crease. Freddie's first three deliveries all narrowly failed to dismiss the Australia captain. After a fortuitous no-ball, however, Flintoff sent down a vicious leg-cutter that caught the outside edge and carried through to Geraint Jones to dismiss Ponting for nought. It had been a phenomenally fast, accurate and threatening over and had turned the game completely. England went on to win the match – narrowly – and the series, with Freddie having proved himself one of the great all-rounders.

Full biography, page 12.

1

A batsman repeatedly asks for a sightscreen to be moved, then hits it when attempting a six. A fielder catches the rebound and appeals, pointing to the sightscreen's wheels which are over the boundary rope and within the field of play. What is your decision?

3 You are umpiring in baking hot conditions. A spin bowler sends down a slow delivery, which fools the striker and hits the wicket. However, although the bails jump up, they land back in position. You refuse the appeal but on close inspection you see that the varnish on the bails has fused them together in the heat. What do you do?

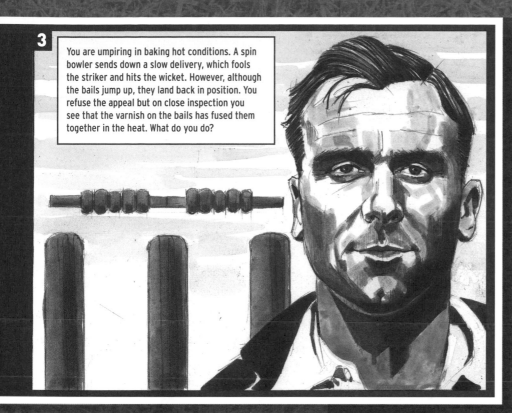

Godfrey Evans

Full name: Thomas Godfrey Evans
Date of birth: August 18, 1920
Major teams: England, Kent

Tests: 91
Ct: 173 St: 46
Ave: 20.49
Centuries: 2
Fifties: 8
High score: 104

One of the finest ever wicketkeepers, Godfrey Evans broke into the England side in 1948 and dominated the position for 13 years. A charismatic figure, he brought fresh attention to an often ignored position, with spectators marvelling as he tumbled and dived, while his dedication and energy inspired his team-mates. Underneath the occasional theatricals, though, was a technically superb keeper: athletic and strong, he had excellent reflexes and quick hands. Above all, he was consistent, with missed chances so scarce that they can be chronicled individually.

He was particularly adept at standing up to fast bowlers, most notably to Alec Bedser, where his positioning had the duel effect of intimidating batsmen and forcing Bedser to bowl the correct line and length. Evans was, before it was a necessary requirement for a keeper, also a more than adequate batsman, with two Test centuries to his name. Consequently he was the first Englishman to reach both 1,000 runs and 100 dismissals and 2,000 runs and 200 dismissals in Test cricket. He was also the first ever wicketkeeper to pass the milestone of 200 Test dismissals. He died in 1999.

2 A pace bowler, having trouble with his run-up, is repeatedly no-balled. When he does take a wicket with a legal delivery he asks you if he can have a practice run-up during the time it takes for the incoming batsman to arrive at the crease. What is your decision?

TREVILLION

3 On a very windy day the bails are repeatedly dislodged by sudden gusts. To put a stop to the distraction, the two captains ask your permission to play with the bails removed. What is your response?

Answers

1) You must award six runs. By law, the sightscreen is always deemed to be outside the boundary.

2) You should allow the bowler to have a practice. The incoming batsman has three minutes to receive the next ball or be ready for his partner to do so, so there is time for the bowler to work on his run-up. Your primary concern in these matters is time-wasting, so here there is no problem.

3) You can allow play to continue without bails – but it's a decision for both umpires alone, not the captains. On windy days you always have the option to use heavier bails, or to remove them altogether.

The Pavilion

THE LAWS OF CRICKET

There are 42 laws of cricket, established by the Marylebone Cricket Club (MCC), the owners of Lord's cricket ground in London. Since their foundation in 1787, the MCC have been the world's sole authority in defining and managing the laws – and only they may change them. This is a brief summary of these 42 laws, covering all the major principles and key decisions.
For the full, official MCC laws, visit www.lords.org

THE SPIRIT

Cricket is a game that owes much of its appeal to the fact that it should be played not only within its laws, but also with the spirit of the game. Any action that is seen to abuse this spirit causes injury to the game itself.

The spirit of the game involves respect for your opponents, your own captain and team, the role of the umpires, and the game's traditional values.

TAKING PART

Law 1. The players. A team consists of 11 players, including a captain.

Law 2. Substitutes. A substitute may be brought on for an injured fielder, but may not bat, bowl, keep wicket or be captain. The replaced player may return if he has recovered. An injured batsman may continue to play with a runner, who completes his runs for him.

Law 3. The umpires. There are two on the pitch, one standing at the bowler's end and the other at square leg. They are responsible for controlling the game as required by the laws, with absolute impartiality. In televised matches, certain decisions can be referred to a third umpire, who has access to replays. The umpires communicate with the players and the scorers using signals *(see pages 112-115).*

Law 4. The scorers. There are two scorers, who respond to the umpires' signals. They must confer regularly.

EQUIPMENT/PITCH

Law 5. The ball. When it is new, the ball shouldn't weigh less than 155.9g or more than 163g, and should have a circumference between 22.4cm and 22.9cm. One ball should be used at a time, and it can only be replaced at the start of each innings, or if it is lost, or if the fielding side request a change after an agreed number of overs.

Law 6. The bat. Bats must be made from wood, not metal, and shouldn't be longer than 96.5cm, or wider than 10.8cm at the widest part. The glove holding the bat is considered part of the bat.

Law 7. The pitch. The pitch is the rectangular part of the ground bounded by bowling creases at either end. It must be 20.12m (originally 22 yards) long and 3.05m wide. The umpires are responsible for determining whether the pitch is in a good enough condition for play.

Law 8. The wickets. There are two sets at either end of the pitch, each made up of three cylindrical wooden stumps, 71.1cm tall. They are placed along the batting crease, equally spaced to form a width of 22.86cm. Two wooden bails are placed on top. The umpires may temporarily dispense with bails if there is high wind. The stumps are known as the off, middle and leg stumps, from left to right as you look at a right-handed batsman.

Law 9. Bowling, popping and return creases. The bowling crease is the line through the centres of the three stumps at each end of the pitch. It is 2.64m long, centred on the middle stump. The popping crease determines whether a batsman is in his ground or not, and determines front-foot no balls. It is 1.22m in front of the bowling crease at each end of the pitch. The return creases are the lines a bowler must be within when delivering, at right angles to the popping crease. The four lines are marked from the popping crease to a minimum of 2.44m behind it.

Law 10. Maintenance of the playing area. The law defines how pitches should be prepared, rolled and maintained.

Law 11. Covering the pitch. The law sets out regulations for covering the pitch in wet conditions, to maintain quality and consistency.

STRUCTURE OF THE GAME

Law 12. Innings. The period during which one side bats. Matches involve either one or two innings, limited by time or by overs. The captain winning the toss decides whether to bat or bowl first. In two-innings games, the sides bat alternately unless the follow-on is enforced (see Law 13). An innings ends when all batsmen are out; when there are no fit batsmen left; the innings is declared or forfeited; or any limit is reached.

Law 13. The follow-on. In a two-innings match, if the side batting second score substantially fewer runs than the side batting first, the first side can force their opponents to bat again immediately. Sides will often take advantage of the follow-on in an attempt to win the match quickly, maintain a psychological advantage against a struggling opponent, or to maintain the momentum of their bowlers. The risk is that if the bowlers tire their opponents may do well in their second innings. For a game of five days or more, the difference must be at least 200 runs. For a three- or four-day game, 150 runs. For a two-day game, 100 runs. For a one-day game, 75 runs.

Sir Alec Bedser, one of
England's greatest players

Law 14. Declaration and forfeiture. The batting captain can choose to declare an innings closed at any time, if the ball is dead. Usually this is because the captain thinks his team have already scored enough runs to win, though sometimes tactical declarations are used in other circumstances. He can also forfeit before the innings has started in order to attempt to force a result.

Law 15. Intervals. The length of lunch, tea and drinks intervals must be agreed before the match begins. The law governs when such breaks may be taken. A drinks break, for instance, may not be taken during the last hour of a match.

Law 16. Start of play, end of play. At the start of a match and after an interval, play begins when the umpire calls 'play'. A session ends with the call 'time', when the bails are removed from both wickets. The last hour of a match must contain at least 20 overs.

Law 17. Practice on the field. Batting and bowling practice on the pitch is forbidden except before the day's play starts, and after it has ended.

SCORING AND WINNING

Law 18. Runs. Runs are scored when the two batsmen run to each other's end of the pitch and make good their ground, when the ball is in play.

Law 19. Boundaries. If the ball touches the boundary or is grounded beyond it – or a fielder, in contact with the ball, touches the boundary or beyond it – a boundary is scored. If the ball hits the ground before a boundary, four runs are scored. If it doesn't touch the ground first, six runs are scored.

Law 20. Lost ball. If a ball in play is lost or cannot be recovered, any fielder can call 'lost ball'. The ball then becomes dead and the batting side retain any penalty runs awarded, and score six runs, or the number of actual runs – whichever is higher. The umpires should replace the ball with one that is in a similar condition to the lost ball.

Law 21. The result. The team who score the most runs wins. If both sides score the same, the match is tied. If the match will run out of time before the innings have been completed, it is drawn.

Law 22. The over. An over is made up of six balls bowled, excluding wides and no balls. Consecutive overs are delivered from opposite ends of the pitch. A bowler may not bowl two overs consecutively.

Law 23. Dead ball. The ball is active when the bowler begins his run-up. It becomes dead when the action from that ball ends. Dead ball is also called if the ball pitches twice and the second pitch lands before the batsman's crease, or in any other case of unfair play or injury. No runs can be scored, or batsmen dismissed, from a dead ball.

Law 24. No ball. Reasons for the umpire calling and signalling a no ball include: the bowler bowling from the wrong place, the bowler straightening his arm once it has reached his shoulder in his delivery, dangerous bowling, or illegally positioned fielders. A no ball adds one run to the batting side's score in addition to any other runs scored from it. The batsmen cannot be out from a no ball apart from through Laws 33, 34, 37 or 38.

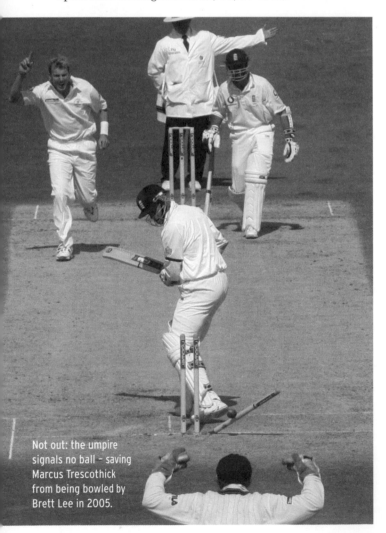

Not out: the umpire signals no ball – saving Marcus Trescothick from being bowled by Brett Lee in 2005.

Law 25. Wide ball. A ball is wide if, in the umpire's opinion, it passes wide of the striker's normal guard position, and he did not have a reasonable chance to score off the ball. A wide adds one run to the batting side's score, in addition to any other runs scored from it. The batsmen cannot be out off a wide apart from through Laws 33, 35, 37, 38 or 39.

Law 26. Bye and leg bye. If a ball that isn't a no ball or a wide passes the batsman without touching his bat or person and runs are scored, they are byes. If the ball hits the batsman but not the bat and runs are scored, they are leg byes. Leg byes can only be scored if the umpire judges that the batsman either tried to play the ball with his bat, or tried to avoid being hit by the ball.

PRINCIPLES OF DISMISSAL

Law 27. Appeals. If fielders believe a batsman is out, they appeal to the umpire with the shout: 'How's That?'. The umpire then makes the decision. Umpires cannot give a batsman out unless there is an appeal.

Law 28. Wicket down. A batsman can be out, subject to Laws 29, 30, 38 and 39, when at least one bail falls as a result of the wicket being hit by the ball, or by the batsman's bat, body or clothing, or by a fielder's hand or arm, if it's the same hand in which he's holding the ball.

Law 29. The batsman is out of his ground. A batsman is out of his ground unless his bat or some part of his person is grounded behind the popping crease at his end. If he is not in his ground, he can be run out or stumped. If both batsmen are stranded in the middle of the pitch, the one closer to the end where the wicket is put down is out.

WAYS TO BE DISMISSED

Law 30. Bowled. A batsman is out if his wicket is put down by a ball delivered by the bowler. The ball may not touch another player or an umpire before doing so.

Law 31. Timed out. An incoming batsman must be ready to face a ball (or be at the crease if he is a non-striker) within three minutes of the outgoing batsman's dismissal. If he is not, the incoming batsman is out.

Law 32. Caught. If a ball hits the bat or the hand holding the bat and is then caught by a fielder before bouncing, the batsman is out.

Law 33. Handled the ball. If a batsman wilfully handles the ball with a hand that is not touching the bat, without the consent of the opposition, he is out, unless it is a genuine attempt to avoid injury.

Law 34. Hit the ball twice. Unless the batsman is trying to protect his wicket or has the opposition's consent, he is out if he hits the ball twice.

Law 35. Hit wicket. If a batsman puts his own wicket down with his bat or his body, clothing or equipment, after the bowler has begun his delivery stride or when starting his first run, and the ball is in play, he is out.

Law 36. Leg before wicket. If the ball hits the batsman without first hitting the bat, but would have hit the wicket if the batsman wasn't there, the batsman is out – but only if the ball does not pitch on the leg side of the wicket. If the ball strikes the batsman outside the line of the off stump, and he was attempting to play a stroke, he is not out. *See full guide, pages 109-111.*

Law 37. Obstructing the field. If a batsman deliberately obstructs the opposition by word or action, he is out.

Law 38. Run out. A batsman is out if, with the ball in play, he is out of his ground and his wicket is fairly put down by the opposing side.

Law 39. Stumped. A batsman is out when the wicketkeeper puts down the wicket, while the batsman is out of his crease and not trying to run.

FIELDING

Law 40. The wicketkeeper. Stands behind the batsman on strike at the wicket to stop balls that pass the batsman, to prevent runs being scored, and to try to dismiss the batsman with a catch, a stumping or a run-out. He is the only fielder allowed to touch the ball with protective gloves.

Law 41. The fielder. There are nine fielders other than the bowler and wicketkeeper. Where they stand is decided by the captain, who may move fielding positions at any time when the ball is dead. *See graphic, page 108.*

Law 42. Fair play. The captains are responsible for ensuring play is conducted within the laws, and within the spirit and traditions of the game. The umpires are the judge of what is not fair play: they may intervene and call the ball dead.

The law covers: a) Ball tampering – deliberately changing the composition of the ball to affect its swing

Sir Garfield Sobers.
Biography, page 71

(other than polishing, which is allowed). b) Distraction – if a fielder deliberately tries to distract a batsman on strike, the ball is dead. For a repeat offence, five penalty runs are awarded. c) Unfair bowling – covers the sustained, deliberate bowling of fast, short balls or high full pitched balls (beamers). If it is deemed dangerous, the umpire calls no ball and cautions the bowler. If it happens a third time in an innings, the bowler is banned from bowling again in that innings and reported to the authorities. d) Time-wasting – any deliberate action from a side playing slowly in an attempt to turn defeat into a draw, or to minimise the number of deliveries, is unfair time-wasting. The umpire will warn the fielding side. If it happens again during an over, the bowler is banned from bowling again in the innings. If it happens outside an over, the batting side are awarded five runs. The side are also reported to the authorities. e) Match fixing.

This is a brief summary of the 42 laws.
For the full, official MCC laws, visit www.lords.org

3rd man

Field placings for a right-handed batsman

Long leg

1st slip

2nd slip

Gully

Leg slip or short fine leg

Wicketkeeper

Square leg

Square leg umpire

Cover point

Silly mid-off

Silly mid-on or forward short leg

Short extra cover

Midwicket

Mid-off

Bowler

Mid-on

Deep extra cover

Umpire

Long-off

Long-on

LBW: GUIDE TO THE LAW

Lbw decisions always cause controversy because the call is a matter of opinion, not fact. They're the hardest calls an umpire has to make because there are so many factors to take into account in a split second. **John Holder** explains what to look out for:

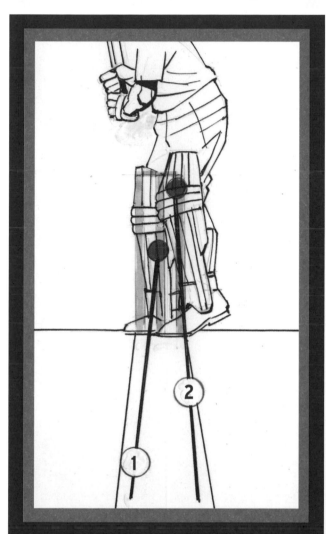

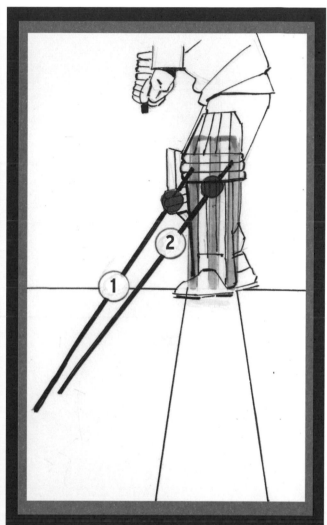

WICKET TO WICKET

1. Out, if you decide the ball would have gone on to hit the wicket.

2. Out, providing the ball would have hit the wicket and not have passed over the stumps.

A fine example of this was Terry Alderman, the Australian fast-medium swing bowler. He bowled very consistently wicket to wicket in the 1989 Ashes series in England and devastated the home side's batsmen, taking 41 wickets.

OFF STUMP

1. If the batsman is hit on the pads outside the line of the off stump, offering no stroke, you can give him out if you judge the ball would have gone on to hit the wicket.

2. Out if you decide the ball would have hit the wicket – ie wouldn't have swung so sharply that it would have passed outside the leg stump.

In the 1992 Test series between England and Pakistan, Waqar Younis used reverse swing to make the ball come back from outside off stump. Many batsmen were either bowled or trapped lbw.

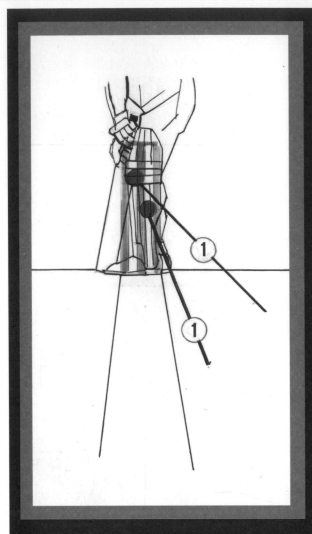

LEG STUMP

1. The batsman cannot be given out lbw to any ball which pitches or makes contact with him outside the line of the leg stump. Batsmen would be at too much of a disadvantage if they could be dismissed by such a delivery.

Shane Warne provides a prime example. In 1993 at Old Trafford his famous delivery to Mike Gatting (page 85) would not have been given out lbw because it pitched outside leg. But then, of course, it turned so sharply it actually hit the off stump – much to Gatting's dismay and everyone else's amazement.

PITCH CONDITIONS

You also need to consider whether the pitch is bouncy or keeping the ball low. When the ball is keeping low, there's less likelihood of it going over the wicket. And when the ball is turning or moving around a great deal, it's more difficult to judge if it would have hit the wicket.

At a 50-over intercontinental match in Rotterdam between Holland and Denmark I ended up giving nine lbws, because the pitch kept so low that the ball repeatedly hit batsmen just above the ankle, making it easier to judge. In contrast, the WACA pitch in Perth is very bouncy and returns few successful lbw decisions.

BOWLER

Also keep an eye on the bowler. A bowler who stands close to the wicket when delivering has a straighter angle to the stumps than one who bowls wide of the crease. The wider the angle of delivery, the more doubt there is about how much the ball is turning, swinging or moving off the pitch.

I umpired Malcolm Marshall dozens of times and he almost invariably delivered the ball from very close to the wicket. As well as being a pleasure to watch in action, his skill in this respect returned many successful lbw appeals.

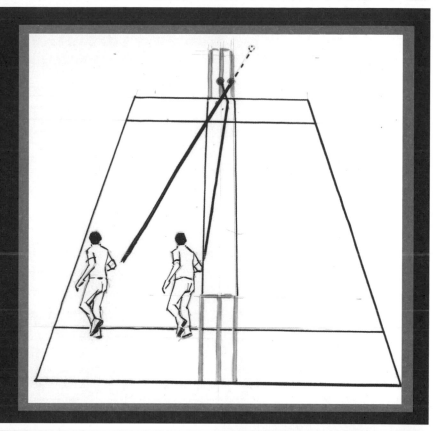

BATSMAN

And you also need to consider the type of batsman when you make your call. Very tall batsmen, like Kevin Pietersen at 6ft 5in, who take a full stride forward are likely to be struck further from the stumps than the likes of Ian Bell, who is around 5ft 10in. The further the point of contact from the stumps, the more doubt there is for you, the umpire, when making the lbw decision.

UMPIRE SIGNALS

Signalling is an integral part of the umpire's role. You need to make it explicitly clear to players, spectators and especially the scorers what has happened on the field of play. Be clear: turn and face the scorers when signalling, and don't allow play to restart until they've acknowledged it. These are the signals you need to know:

Out The classic pose. Raise your arm and extend your index finger upwards. Some umpires like to hold their arm in front of them – I prefer to hold it to the side of my head.

No ball Extend either arm horizontally at a right angle to your body. Some umpires face their palm up, I prefer to face mine down. You should also call 'no ball'.

Leg byes Given when the ball beats the bat, but strikes the batsman's body when he is playing a shot and runs are scored. Raise either leg so your foot is off the ground, extend either arm and tap the raised leg repeatedly.

Four runs Extend either arm horizontally in front of the body and move it from left to right in a waving motion. At the end of the signal the arm should be in front of the body.

Six runs Raise both arms above the head with fingers outstretched. It's the signal that delights spectators, ensures a grin from the batsman and a grimace from the bowler.

Byes When the ball beats the bat, misses the striker's body and the wicketkeeper, and runs are scored, they count as byes. Extend your arm vertically, your palm facing forwards and your fingers outstretched.

Dead ball
Bend forward and cross your arms repeatedly with your fingers pointing downwards in front of your thighs. It's awkward, but it tells the scorers and the players that there can be no further actions relating to that ball. Also call 'dead ball'.

Five penalty runs
Rest your hand on your shoulder when awarding five penalty runs to the fielding side. For the batting side, your hand pats your shoulder.

Revoking the last signal
Like the penalty runs signal, this one was new in 2000. Cross both arms across your chest with the palms down on opposite shoulders. In the case of a dismissal, for example, if you change your decision, you would recall the batsman verbally and then make this signal to the scorers.

Short run
Although rarely used because short runs occur very infrequently, it's still an important part of your signalling armoury and umpires should always be alert for batsmen running short. Either arm may be used. Reach up and pat the top of the same arm's shoulder repeatedly. You should also call 'short run'.

New ball This one is obvious enough. It's simply an indication that the fielding side has taken the new ball. Raise the ball above your head vertically so players and scorers can all see it and say 'new ball'.

Last hour Introduced in 2000, this signal is intended to stop time wasting by either side. The signal lets the players know there is one hour left and they now have a specific minimum number of overs to be completed. Raise your arm, point at your watch and call 'last hour'.

Wide ball Extend both arms simultaneously at right angles from the body, with fingers outstretched. The palms can be facing in any direction and you should also call 'wide ball'. Calling balls wide tends to be more strict in limited overs cricket to try deter negative bowling.

THE STORY OF THE SPORT

WHERE AND WHEN DID CRICKET BEGIN?

It's a question which may never be fully answered. An ancient game, cricket has a number of possible roots, some in England, others in India and Persia. But most experts agree that the likeliest answer is that the modern sport emerged from the Weald area of south-east England in the 16th century. A rural pastime, it was played by shepherds using curved crooks (the Anglo-Saxon word 'cricce' or 'crycc', means stick) and involved protecting a wicket-gate from a crudely made rolling 'ball'.

But it's far from an exact history. In 1180 Joseph of Exeter wrote a couplet reading: 'The youths at crick did play/Throughout the merry day.' And the 1300 Wardrobe Accounts of Edward I refer to the teenage Prince of Wales playing 'creag'. But most believe that, although accounts such as these refer to games similar to modern cricket, it was in the Weald – which stretches across Surrey, Sussex and Kent – where the recognisable game began.

The first definite reference to cricket is in 1598, when a man named John Derrick testified in court that: 'Being a scholar in the free school of Guildford he and diverse of his fellows did runne and play there at cricket and plaies.' At the time of his statement, Derrick was around 60 – so he would have been playing cricket in the 1550s.

GRISLY EVIDENCE

Much of the early evidence of the emergence of cricket comes from court records. In 1611 two men in Sussex were fined and ordered to pay penance for playing cricket on a Sunday rather than attending church. And in 1624, a coroner's jury investigated a case in which Jasper Vinall was killed after being hit by a wild swipe from a bat while trying to catch the ball. Cases such as these all centred on the counties of Surrey, Sussex and Kent.

ETON AND OXFORD

But that changed in the 18th century, as the sport began to develop from a rural, lower-orders sport into one played and sponsored by the wealthy. William Goldwin's poem *In Certamen Pilae* refers to cricket being played at the top public school Eton by the 1690s, and by 1729 Samuel Johnson was playing the sport at Oxford. Much of this boom was led by gambling: rich young aristocrats staged matches to bet on the outcome, attracting spectators and press coverage. A document from 1706 indicates that, by then, there was a widely shared understanding of the sport's essential ingredients: two batsmen, a bowler and two stumps with a bail.

An early depiction of a London cricket match from 1743

Action from 1780: cricket being played at the White Conduit House in London's Islington, the original home of the MCC.

THE LAWS

As the players became better educated and the money involved grew, there was a clear need for a complete, uniform set of laws. The first known version was issued by the London Club in 1744, specifying, among other rules, that the pitch must be 22 yards long. These were revised in 1774 by 'Noblemen and Gentlemen' at the Star and Garter pub in London's Pall Mall.

In 1756 the Hambledon Cricket Club had been founded. Hambledon in Hampshire had a huge influence on the development of the modern sport: purifying batting techniques, popularising airborne bowling, introducing straight-bladed bats and using a third stump. But by 1787 it had been overtaken by the current keepers of cricket: Lord's and the Marylebone Cricket Club. Thomas Lord, a player from Yorkshire, founded his club in what is now Dorset Square, near Baker Street station in London. At the same time, the MCC were established and, by the following year, were powerful enough to revise the laws. Gradually, these laws became the most widely adopted. Today, the MCC remain the custodians of the laws, based at their home since 1814 in St John's Wood.

THE NEW GAME

The rules of 1774 had prompted a change in bowling technique. In the sport's earliest days, bowling was underarm and along the ground. The 1744 codification, however, narrowed but heightened the stumps, encouraging length bowling, where the bowler flights the ball so that it pitches and bounces. This in turn led to changes in batting technique: bats were straightened, batsmen started to hit the ball with a vertical rather than a horizontal swing, off-side shots were introduced and defensive shots were used.

And the laws remained fluid, responding to the way the sport developed. Professional bowlers in the 19th century began to bowl round-arm, flouting the MCC's laws, so by 1835 the MCC were forced to adapt the laws to allow the technique. And by 1864 – the year WG Grace made his Lord's debut, aged 16 (see page 22) – the MCC were again compelled to change the laws by accepting over-arm bowling. Equipment developed, too, as safety conscious players took to using cork pads and thick gloves to protect themselves from injury.

GOING NATIONAL...

Cricket grew and grew in England in the 19th century, helped by the spread of railways. It had become a major spectator sport and in 1864 a haphazard County Championship was held, featuring eight sides. At a meeting in London in 1873 rules were written for the creation of a formal championship with initially nine counties – Derbyshire, Gloucestershire, Kent, Lancashire, Middlesex, Nottinghamshire, Surrey, Sussex and Yorkshire

Above: Lord's in 1825

Below: The England cricket team on tour in North America in 1859

– and the MCC were appointed the arbitrators in case of disagreement. The format was tightened in 1890, with eight teams. The number of 'first-class' counties continued to increase until 1991 when Durham joined, bringing the figure to 18.

... AND INTERNATIONAL

In 1877, starting on 15 March, England played Australia at the Melbourne Cricket Ground in what has became recognised as the first Test match, with the home team winning by 45 runs. While a team that styled themselves 'All England' played Kent in 1739, the true roots of the modern side were in 1846 when William Clark, a one-eyed professional cricketer, formed the first All-England team. In 1852, a rival England side, the United All-England XI, was formed by John Wisden, with the two sides meeting in an annual fixture. In 1859 the two teams combined under the captaincy of George Parr and toured North America, where they won all five of their matches.

Surprisingly, the first match contested between two countries did not feature England at all, but was held between Canada and the United States in New York in 1844. Cricket remained one of the most popular sports in

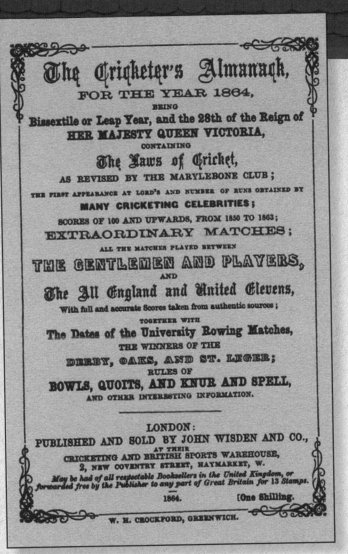

John Wisden's first yearbook, The Cricketer's Almanack, published in 1864

America until the outbreak of the Civil War, after which baseball was dominant.

England remained the heart of cricket. The popularity of Test matches was consolidated in 1882, with the creation of the Ashes. After Australia's victory at The Oval – England's first defeat on home soil – a fake obituary for English cricket was published in the Sporting Times, concluding: 'The body will be cremated and the ashes taken to Australia.' During the following winter's tour of Australia, a group of women presented the now famous urn to England captain Ivo Bligh, to symbolise the ashes. So began one of the oldest and fiercest rivalries in world sport.

Cricket had been spread around the globe through the power and reach of the British Empire. In 1841 General Lord Hill decreed that every barracks should possess a cricket ground. But the British had no need to impose the sport: just as it had in England, cricket proved remarkably popular. After England and Australia, South Africa joined the Test fold in 1889, followed by West Indies in 1928, New Zealand in 1930, India in 1932, Pakistan in 1952, Sri Lanka in 1982 and Bangladesh in 2000.

THE EVOLVING FORMATS

Early Test cricket didn't have the same form as today, with the first five-day Test not taking place until 1948 in England, and declarations (at any time of the captain's choosing) not authorised until 1957. In 1947 the Imperial Cricket Conference (ICC) formalised the term 'first-class cricket' for the first time – a match of three or more days' duration between two sides of 11 players of sufficient quality. And limited-overs cricket also began to appear: in 1963 the Gillette Cup, the first significant limited-overs tournament, was established in England. This was followed, in 1971, with the first one-day international, with 50 overs played per side: just as in the first Test, Australia beat England at Melbourne, in a match staged due to rain ruining a five-day match. The new format proved a success and the World Cup was inaugurated in 1975.

TODAY – AND BEYOND

In the late 1970s, the sport was shaken up by World Series Cricket, a competition formed by Australian entrepreneur Kerry Packer. It lured top cricketers away from established international cricket with huge salary increases, and the tournament briefly threatened to cause a schism in the sport. WSC introduced many features that survive to this day: higher wages, night matches and coloured clothing (below). And in 2003 another new form of cricket was created in England: Twenty20, in which sides face 20 overs. The format was an immediate hit with spectators: international matches –- the first between Australia and New Zealand in 2005 – and a world championship soon followed.

What the future holds for the sport is unclear. In 2008 the Indian Premier League was formed, on the Twenty20 format, while a one off match between England and a West Indies team involved the winners receiving $1m a player. This ability to evolve over time seems to guarantee that the sport will continue to delight players and spectators for years to come.

THE BEGINNINGS

The evolution of the bat reveals a lot about the sport's origins. Shaped like shepherd's crooks or hockey sticks, the early bats were long, heavy clubs, designed to face underarm bowling. The ball was rolled fast along the ground, so the curve helped batsmen scoop it into the air. What is believed to be the oldest surviving bat – on display at The Oval – dates from 1729 (below).

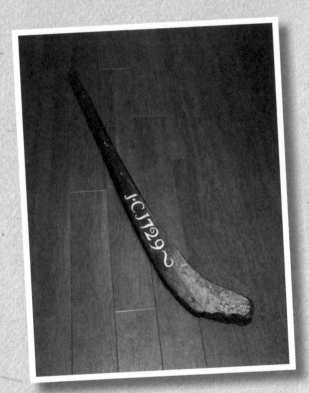

NEW CHALLENGES

By the 1820s round-arm bowling was allowed, resulting in more bounce and greater speed. So, to cope, bats became lighter, with a higher swell. In the 1830s, as bowling became still faster and more powerful, bat-makers began to splice separate handles (made of ash or willow) into bats to make them stronger. In the following two decades, springs were added, as were handles with India rubber grips. In 1835, the length of a bat was limited at 38 inches – again, the same applies today.

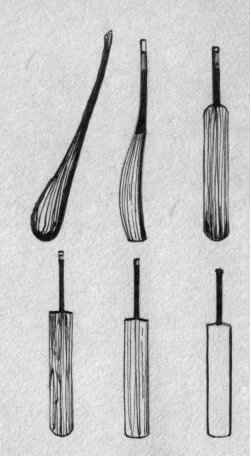

STRAIGHTENING UP

But with the first laws of cricket in 1744 came comprehensive change. The stumps were narrowed but heightened, encouraging (still underarm) length bowling. In response, bats evolved, growing straighter so that batsmen could hit the pitching ball with a vertical rather than a horizontal bat, allowing off-side and defensive shots. And by the 1750s the bat had begun to take its modern shape.

CONTROLLING THE SIZE

In 1771, the first laws governing the size of a bat were introduced, after a batsman called Thomas White walked on to the field in a game between Reigate and Hambledon carrying a two-foot wide bat – as wide as the stumps. It was a cunning plan: he scored 197. But it also ruined the game. The new law stated that the bat should not be wider than 4.25 inches – a definition that survives today.

OVERARM BOWLING

But the biggest new challenge for the bat was the introduction of over-arm bowling in 1864. The bat needed to be lighter, straight, with a flat face, a high swell, a spliced handle and a rubber grip. In 1890, English bat maker CC Bussey began producing bats from the willow's light sapwood (instead of the traditional heartwood), reducing the weight from around 5lb to 2lb. It made for stylish, attractive stroke-play. Bats remained light until the 1960s, when players such as Clive Lloyd upped the weight to around 3lb, producing more power.

THE METAL MOMENT

But attempts to increase power haven't always been successful. In December 1979 Australia's Dennis Lillee turned up at the WACA Ground in Perth to face England carrying an aluminium bat (pictured right). There was nothing in the laws to stop him – but both sides objected: England because it was unsporting and would damage the ball; Australia because captain Greg Chappell believed the bat wouldn't work. After a row, Lillee did change – and a few months later, the laws were amended to state bats must always be wooden.

TODAY'S BAT

Attempts to perfect the modern bat, within the Laws, continue. In the 1970s manufacturer Gray Nicolls introduced the Super Scoop, which had a large hollow at the back and additional wood around the edges. This redistributed the weight to the edge, increasing the size of the sweet spot. Similar experiments have helped create a generation of modern bats with large and forgiving sweet spots, encouraging adventurous, attacking batting, and increasing run-rates. It's all a long way from those shepherd's crooks…

England's Kevin Pietersen in action

THE BEGINNINGS

With cricket emerging from rural, poor communities, the earliest balls were nothing fancy: stones, lumps of coiled wool (possibly matted with red wax), pine cones or roughly sculpted wood – in fact, anything that would roll and could be hit. The first known reference to a properly manufactured ball comes in 1658: interlaced strips of hide stuffed with feathers or cloth. And in 1706 a poem by William Goldwin refers to cricket being played with a 'leathern sphere' – a sign of what was to come.

A ball used in the Bodyline series in 1932-33, with the mount signed by players including Douglas Jardine and Harold Larwood. (See p42 and 66)

THE ROYAL PATENT

The ball gradually developed through the latter-half of the 17th century. In 1775, Duke and Son of Kent produced the first six-seamer, which won a royal patent from the Prince of Wales – and passed the new standardisation test: the world's first club, Hambledon, stipulating a year earlier that 'the ball must not weigh less than five ounces and a half, no more than five ounces and three quarters'. John Small of Petersfield made similar balls for Hambledon and the MCC.

THE SURVIVOR

The oldest surviving ball – known after the MCC regular, William Ward, who spent three days in bat with it at Lord's scoring 278 – dates from 1820. With a core of cork, encased in two halves of tanned hide and hand-sewn, it was red – possibly like the original waxed wool balls. Cricket balls stayed red until Kerry Packer introduced white balls under the floodlights at Sydney during the second year of World Series Cricket in 1978-79. There have also been experiments with yellow, orange and pink balls since.

THE SIZE

On 10 May 1838 the Marylebone Cricket Club decreed that the ball should have a circumference of between 9 and 9.25 inches. In 1927 the law was amended to between 8.81 and 9 inches.

MAKING THE MODERN BALL

The modern form and method of manufacture dates back to 1853. Each ball takes around 75 days to make. They start life as a small greyish ball of cork-rubber. This is then wrapped first in small strips of cork, followed by a layer of wet woollen string. Once that's done, it is beaten into shape – then the process is repeated four more times. The final core is hung to dry for two-and-a-half months.

The leather shell, meanwhile, is made from four pointed leather ovals. The quarters are split into pairs, turned inside out and sewn together. Then, after an additional layer of thin leather is wrapped around the core, these halves are turned right side out and pressed together with steel cups. The ball is then closed by expert lip-stitchers, using seam thread strengthened with animal fat, creating a total of six rows of stitches. It's a process used worldwide – though balls made in England are also coated with a resinous oil mixture to protect them against the rain. The best balls cost around £80 each – and for Test matches, each must be used for a minimum of 80 overs.

From slab of stone to the three stump wicket

THE BEGINNINGS

The earliest wickets were improvised: the shepherds who played early forms of the sport using either basic countryside gates as their targets ('wiket' being the Middle English word for gate), or the stumps of trees – explaining the modern term. When wickets began to be made specifically for cricket, they went through various different styles, as shown below. Most used only two stumps, a ball's width apart, ranging in height from around 12 to 22 inches. But the 1744 codification of the Laws resulted in the size being fixed for the first time – 22 inches high, and six inches wide – and in the mandatory use of bails.

THE MIDDLE STUMP

In a match in May 1775, Lumpy Stevens, one of the finest bowlers of his day, beat his batsman three times, but the ball passed between the two stumps, failing to dislodge the bails. From then on a third, middle stump was introduced. The three stumps came to be known as the middle stump, the off stump (on the side of the player's bat) and the leg stump (on the batsman's leg-side). In 1798 the dimensions changed again: 23 inches tall and seven inches wide – with a further inch added to the width in 1820. And in 1931, they grew again to the size they are today: 28 inches tall, and nine inches wide.

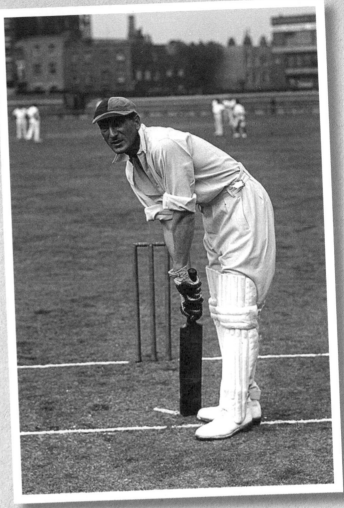

Douglas Jardine in 1929

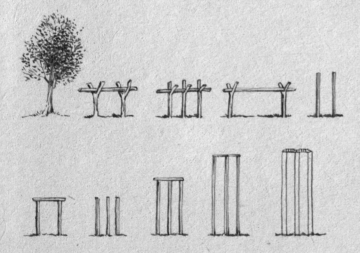

THE EXCEPTIONS

But this being cricket, there were plenty of other more bizarre incarnations. In 1794, a Catholic school for English boys founded in the Low Countries ended 200 years of exile from religious persecution by becoming Stonyhurst College, and brought with them from Liege their unique brand of cricket – one that had developed in isolation. The students of Stonyhurst used only one wicket – a large slab of stone, 17in tall and 13in broad. And in 1834, in a famous Lord's match dubbed 'The Barn-Door Match' between the Gentlemen and the Players, the Gentlemen used wickets 35 inches tall and 12 wide. They had endured 20 years of defeats, during which they used tactics like taking to the field with 17 men in an effort to force a victory – so they hoped these colossal wickets would help them win. It was a decent idea – but they still lost by an innings.

TODAY'S WICKETS

The rules today are specific: the two sets of wickets must be placed opposite each other at a distance of 22 yards between the two middle stumps. Each set must be 9 inches (22.86 cm) wide and the top of the stumps must be 28in (71.1cm) above the playing surface. The top of modern stumps are dome shaped, except for the grooves for the bails, while the rest of the stump must be cylindrical. Each wicket must have three wooden stumps and two wooden bails.

DRAW LIKE THE EXPERT

Artist Paul Trevillion explains how he creates one of his unique You Are The Umpire strips

1. The first stage is getting the likeness bang on. I start with a preliminary drawing twice the size of the actual final artwork so I can check the eye, nose and mouth proportions, and make sure I'm happy with how it's looking.

3. Then I begin the detailed work of the actual drawing that goes into the strip (five and a half inches high) as a basic pencil outline. At this stage you can see I've included the year 1948 on Bradman's hat, just beneath the Australian badge.

2. On the same drawing I apply vertical line shading, which gives the face depth and contours – this really helps me confirm whether or not I've captured the subject. I like to have the right atmosphere in my studio when I'm working: when I'm doing cricket I always have the Ashes urn on my working board. If it's football, I have a *Sunday Express* from 1966 signed by the World Cup-winning team by my elbow. And if it's boxing, the glove signed by Oscar de la Hoya. It helps add an air of excitement when I draw and paint.

4. As before, here I apply the vertical-line shading to the real drawing, which starts to bring it to life. I'm not fussy which pencils I use to draw – anything with a lead. It's the same with the brush. As long as it's got a few hairs I'm happy! It's the pen that does the work. I've used the Guillot 290 ink nib for 50 years, but they're becoming harder and harder to find. Pen and ink work is a lost art. Although for the masters such as Rembrandt and Da Vinci, it was one of their favourite mediums.

5. At this stage, as you can see, I take a step back from the main subject and work on other parts of the strip. This allows me to clear my head and return to the portrait with a fresh perspective later. If the light is good a piece of work is generally a 24-hour turnaround. By that I mean there are times when the drawing takes two hours and I'm satisfied I've captured the player's personality. But there are other times when it becomes a challenge and morning becomes night before it's finished. If I had to name just one drawing in this book which is my special favourite, for example, it would be the head of Wally Hammond (page 30). I got it right first time!

7. I work in inks and here I'm applying the final heavy ink wash – after which there's no chance to change the work. It has to be right, and I have to be fully committed and happy with the drawing at this point. I use Windsor & Newton inks. But once applied it's permanent – there's no going back. It's not like working in oils, where you can continually change and correct. Working in ink is the ultimate challenge. You have to get it right first time. This is what adds to the excitement of the work. It gives it life.

6. Now it's time to apply the first colour wash. In this case I decided that I'd actually remove the '1948' from the cap because I felt it distracted attention away from Bradman's face. I always have the radio on when I work. Radio 5 Live for the sport. But at 5pm on a Saturday when the Sports Report signature tune sounds out, I always stop work and listen for an hour.

8. With the main subject complete I ink in the rest of the final frame in colour and the strip is finished. The final touch is signing it. On the advice of my art teacher at school – 'It's Rembrandt, Michelangelo, Picasso – just one name' – I've only ever signed my work 'TREVILLION'…!

TREVILLION

QUIZ

Over 1: GROUNDS FOR DEBATE

1. Which ground hosted the first Test held in England?

2. An English ground hosted its first Test in 1884 - but it started a day late because of rain. Which ground?

3. Which current League football ground hosted a Test match in 1902, but never staged another?

4. Which Australian city first hosted a Test in 1970?

5. The Oval is in Kennington, London. Where is the Kensington Oval?

6. Eden Gardens and Eden Park - Test venues in which cities?

FACT

4: number of deliveries in an over in England between 1880-1888. From 1890-1899 this became five, before six-ball overs were introduced in 1900. (In 1922 Australia introduced an eight-ball over, which spread to New Zealand and South Africa, and, for one year only - 1939 - to England.) Since 1979 the six-ball over has been used worldwide.

The boundary rope didn't exist until 1865. Until then, batsmen scored by completing runs, or by hitting a six out of the playing area. But during a match at Lord's in 1865, Lancashire opener AN Hornby was fielding in the deep, and had to chase a high ball into the crowd around the pitch. In doing so, he ran into an old man, who fell and was badly hurt. Soon afterwards Lord's introduced the boundary rope - and other grounds followed suit.

Over 2: GETTING RESULTS

1. What was unusual about Australia v West Indies at Brisbane in 1960, and India v Australia at Madras in 1986?

2. In 1977, Australia won the Centenary Test in Melbourne against England by 45 runs. What was so unusual about this margin?

3. England - at Sydney in 1894 and Headingley in 1981 - have beaten Australia twice after following on. Which team managed this feat in 2001?

4. Middlesex (1975) and Northamptonshire (1987) are the only counties to record what unfortunate double?

5. This team played their first Test in 1930, but did not win one for 44 matches - till 1956. Which country?

6. Brian Lara hit two record Test scores and one record first-class score. How many of those matches did his team win?

Over 3: ONE-DAY FIRSTS

1. England's first one-day county competition started as 65 overs per side in 1963, but had five overs per team shaved off from 1964 onwards. Who were its initial sponsors?

2. Who scored the first century in a one-day county final?

3. England played Australia in the first one-day international, in Melbourne in January 1971. Why was the match arranged?

4. The first World Cup was in England in 1975. Which famous Indian player batted 60 overs for 36 runs in his side's opening game?

5. Who scored a century when West Indies won the first World Cup final?

6. Which South African became the first player to hit six sixes in an over in a one-day international during the 2007 World Cup?

Over 4: FAMILY AFFAIRS

1. Three of batsman Vic Richardson's grandsons also played for Australia - who?

2. For decades she was the only woman to appear in Wisden's list of the births and deaths of cricketers, because she taught three sons - one especially - to play the game. Who was she?

3. The father of Dayle and Sir Richard Hadlee also played Tests for New Zealand, captaining their 1949 tour to England. What was his name?

4. The grandfather played 22 Tests for West Indies in a career ruined by the Second World War, the son played two Tests for them, the grandson played 15 Tests for England. Name the trio.

5. Shoaib played Test cricket for Pakistan - so did his father and three uncles. Name them.

6. His father captained England then his godfather, as chairman of selectors, chose him to captain England in 1988. Who?

Over 5: ENGLAND'S BORN CAPTAINS

1. Kevin Pietersen was born in South Africa. Who was the last England captain born there?

2. The father of England captain Ted Dexter founded a club called the MCC - in his son's birthplace. Which city?

3. England captains Douglas Jardine and Colin Cowdrey were born in which country?

4. In spells between 1972 and 1975, England were captained by a Welshman and a Scotsman. Who?

5. Which England one-day captain of the 1990s was born in Australia?

6. Michael Vaughan was born in which first-class county?

Over 6: GONE BUT NOT FORGOTTEN

1. England's 1980-81 tour to the West Indies was overshadowed by the death of which popular coach?

2. Which cricket figure died in room 374 of the Jamaica Pegasus Hotel?

3. Which West Indies star of the 1980s died aged just 41 in 1999?

4. Andy Ducat (1886-1942) is famous for dying where?

5. He took 15 wickets for 104 runs the last time England beat Australia in a Test at Lord's, then was killed during the Allied invasion of Sicily in 1943. Which Yorkshire spinner?

6. Who is the only Test cricketer to be executed?

Over 7: UMPIRES

1. Which umpire was famous for standing on one leg when the score was on the "unlucky number" 111, or 222, 333 etc?

2. What is the real first name of former umpire Dickie Bird?

3. Indian Test umpire Srinivasaraghavan Venkataraghavan was better known as what?

4. Umpire Edmund Barton helped quell a riot in protest at his fellow umpire's decision when New South Wales played an England XI in 1879. The popularity he gained set him on the road to what other job?

5. Which umpire was involved in a famous stand-off with England captain Mike Gatting in 1987, leading to the loss of a day's play between the touring team and Pakistan?

6. Which Test umpire, who suffers from arthritis, gives players out with a crooked finger rather than a straight one?

ANSWERS

1. GROUNDS FOR DEBATE
1) The Oval, in 1880
2) Old Trafford, Manchester
3) Sheffield United's Bramall Lane
4) Perth
5) Bridgetown, Barbados
6) Kolkata and Auckland

2. GETTING RESULTS
1) These are the only Test matches to end in ties
2) Australia had also won the very first Test, in 1877, by 45 runs
3) India at Kolkata. These three are the only Tests won by a team following on
4) To lose two one-day Lord's finals in one season
5) New Zealand
6) None - they were all draws

3. ONE-DAY FIRSTS
1) Gillette
2) Geoffrey Boycott, 146 for Yorkshire against Surrey in the 1965 Gillette Cup final
3) The Test had been washed out for three days, leading to an abandonment, so the sides played a 40-over game on the scheduled fifth day

4. FAMILY AFFAIRS
1) Ian, Greg and Trevor Chappell
2) Martha Grace, mother of Fred, Edward and of course WG Grace
3) Walter
4) George, Ron and Dean Headley
5) Hanif (Shoaib's father), Wazir, Mushtaq and Sadiq Mohammad
6) Chris Cowdrey, son of Colin, godson of Peter May

5. ENGLAND'S BORN CAPTAINS
1) Allan Lamb
2) Milan, Italy
3) India - as was Nasser Hussain
4) Tony Lewis and Mike Denness
5) Adam Hollioake
6) Lancashire - and but for a rule change he would never have been able to play for Yorkshire, where he moved when he was nine

6. GONE BUT NOT FORGOTTEN
1) Ken Barrington, who had played 82 Tests
2) Pakistan coach Bob Woolmer in March 2007
3) Malcolm Marshall
4) On the pitch at Lord's, of a heart attack during a wartime match
5) Hedley Verity
6) West Indies' Leslie Hylton, who murdered his wife and was executed in 1955

7. UMPIRES
1) David Shepherd
2) Harold
3) Venkat
4) Prime minister of Australia - he became an MP the same year as the riot
5) Shakoor Rana
6) Billy Bowden

GLOSSARY

Arm ball: A ball bowled by an off-spinner or a slow left-arm orthodox bowler which doesn't turn and goes straight on. Also known as a **floater**.

Block hole: The area between the batsman's feet and his bat (when waiting to receive a delivery). So called because a delivery which lands there blocks the batsman's ability to play shots. A good **yorker** will land in the block hole.

Bouncer: A delivery that pitches short and flies into the body or towards the head of the batsman. Also called a **bumper**.

Bunsen: A pitch that is likely to turn and, therefore, favours spin bowling. It's rhyming slang, from 'bunsen burner'.

Charge: A batsman moving down the wicket out of his crease and towards the bowler in an attempt to change the pitch of the ball. If the batsman is particularly nimble or classical, or is facing slow bowling, he **dances** down the wicket.

Cherry: A colloquial term for a cricket ball, often used when the ball is new.

Chinaman: Left-arm unorthodox spin. Bowled over the wrist, the ball turns from off to leg (for a right-handed batsman).

Chinese cut: An accidental shot, in which the ball catches the inside edge of the bat, goes behind the batsman – missing the stumps – and runs away for runs. Also known as a **French cut**.

Chucker: A bowler with an illegal or suspect action, where he fails to keep the bend of his arm within the legal parameters.

Collapse: The loss of multiple wickets for minimal runs, often after a promising start. As perfected by the England middle order.

Corridor of uncertainty: The area outside off stump where the batsman is undecided whether to hit or to leave the ball. Coined by Geoffrey Boycott.

Cow corner: The region of the field roughly between deep mid-wicket and long-on. So named because a shot which ends up there is **agricultural** – an unsophisticated attacking shot – and because, given the absence of fielders, cows could graze there undisturbed. A shot that goes to cow corner is a **cow shot**.

Dab: A gentle late cut.

Daisy-cutter: A ball that bounces more than once before reaching the batsman, or one which is rolled along the ground, or which hardly bounces.

Danger end: The end of the pitch most likely to be targeted for a run-out while batsmen are attempting a run.

Declaration: When the batting team's captain believes that it would be strategically preferable to end the innings, he can **declare** and force his opponents to bat.

Dolly: A very easy, gentle catch. Also called a **sitter**.

Doosra: An off-spinner's **googly**, the doosra spins from leg to off (for a right-handed batsman). The term means 'the other one' or 'the second one' in Urdu and Hindi.

Dorothy: Australian slang for a six. It's rhyming slang derived form 'Dorothy Dix', a US agony aunt.

Dot ball: A delivery from which no runs are scored. Six dot balls in an over is a **maiden over**.

Duck: When a batsman is dismissed without scoring a run. If he's dismissed with the first ball faced it's a **golden duck**. Two ducks in a match is a **pair**. Two golden ducks in a match is a **king pair**.

Edge: When a delivery clips the side or corner of the bat, often resulting in a catch or a chance. A batsman is said to have **edged** the ball. If the ball clips the edge nearest the batsman's legs it's an **inside edge**; if it clips the edge furthest from the batsman it's an **outside edge**. If it hits the front edge of the bat, when a player is attempting a cross-bat shot, it's a **leading edge**. Also called a **snick** or a **nick** and a batsman may **feather** the ball.

Farm: To control the strike, particularly by scoring a single near the end of each over. Used when a recognised batsman is playing with a tail-ender and wants to face the majority of balls himself. Also known as to **shepherd** the strike.

Fifer: When a bowler has taken five or more wickets in an innings. Also called a **five-for**, a **five-fer**, a **five-wicket haul**, or a **Michelle** (after actress Michelle Pfieffer).

Fishing: When a batsman **hangs out his bat** unwisely in an attempt to hit the ball or **throws his bat** at a wider delivery.

Flat-track bully: A player who thrives against mediocre opposition or when the conditions favour batting – with the implication that he struggles in tougher circumstances.

Flipper: A wrist spinner's delivery with limited bounce.

Flog: To score many runs very quickly off a bowler. A bowler is **flogged**, often **all over the park**.

Full toss: A delivery that reaches the batsman without bouncing first. A **beamer** is a head-high full toss.

Googly: A delivery, bowled by a right-armed leg-spinner, that spins from off to leg. Also called a **Bosie** (after its inventor, Bernard Bosanquet) and, particularly in Australia, a **wrong 'un**.

Half-volley: A ball that bounces just short of the block hole and results in an easy shot for the batsman.

Hat-trick: When a bowler takes three wickets with three consecutive deliveries.

Hook: A cross-battted shot played at a shoulder or head-high ball. A **hooker** is a player with a propensity for playing the hook shot.

Jaffa: An extremely good delivery, which either took a wicket or deserved to. Normally applied to a fast bowler. Also called a **corker**.

Knock: An individual batsman's innings. While a batsman can have a **good knock**, the term is normally applied to scores of less than a hundred.

Line and length: Bowling that pitches just outside off stump and on a good length. Suggests that a bowler is concentrating on accuracy and consistency, rather than special wicket-taking balls.

Metronome: A reliable, accurate and dangerous bowler. Such a player's bowling would be **metronomic**. There's the implication that the bowler focuses on bowling the correct **line and length** and on **landing the ball in the right places**.

Mullygrubber: A ball that randomly fails to bounce and keeps low. Coined by Richie Benaud. Also called, among other terms, an **ankle-grabber**, a **scuttler**, a **sneaker** and a **torpedo**.

Nelson: A score of 111 (either by an individual or a team) and often considered unlucky. 222 is a **Double Nelson** and 333 a **Triple Nelson**.

Nightwatchman: A player, normally a bowler, who has been promoted up the batting order to protect more recognised batsman from a difficult period of play. Often used near the end of a day's play.

Nudge: An unambitious shot, probably a push, which results in only one or two runs. A batsman who moves the ball around, scoring in singles, rather than hitting boundaries can be said to **nudge and nurdle**, suggesting a lack of elegance. A player who **nudges and nurdles** is an **accumulator**. If he's also hard to get out, the batsman is **nuggety**.

Pinch hitter: A player at the top of order with the designated role of scoring at as high a rate as possible. Often a hard-hitting lower-order batsman promoted up the order. A term borrowed from baseball.

Play and miss: When a batsman attempts but fails to hit the ball. Never applies to a situation when a wicket has been taken. The bowler, or the ball, can be said to have **beaten the bat**.

Plumb: A definite and clear lbw decision.

Pull: A cross-batted shot played at a waist-high ball. Unlike with the **hook** shot, the batsman rolls his wrists in an attempt to keep the ball down.

Reverse sweep: A sweep in which the batsman switches his stance and hands to effectively bat with the opposite hand – that is, a right-handed batsman will play the shot as if left-handed.

Rib Tickler: A rising ball that hits the batsman in the ribs. The delivery probably **got big** on the batsman.

Shooter: A delivery that skids on pitching, speeds up and keeps low. Similar to a **mullygrubber**.

Skier: A ball that a batsman has mishit and has gone directly up in the air. A ball deliberately hit very high is an **air hostess**.

Sledging: The art of verbally insulting or mocking your opponent in an effort to distract or goad him.

Slider: A delivery bowled by a wrist-spin bowler with the thumb facing the bowler, resulting in backspin. The delivery is on a full length, has limited bounce and goes straight on rather than turning.

Slog: An aggressive and probably ungainly shot in which the batsman swings the bat and attempts to hit the ball as far as possible, generally in the air. A batsman who frequently **slogs** is a **slogger**. A **hoik**, a **heave** and an **agricultural shot** are all types of slog.

Sticky wicket: An archaic term for when wet uncovered pitches dried, resulting in variable bounce and turn. Today it refers to a wet wicket, or a situation which is difficult or unpredictable.

Straight: Bowlers are urged to bowl directly at the batsman's wicket – that is, **wicket to wicket** – under the theory that you miss, I hit. However if a bowler is said to bowl **straight up and down** – without swing, spin or seam – it's considered an insult.

Strike bowler: A bowler who is his side's designated wicket-taker, **spearhead**, or fastest bowler. Strike bowlers often bowl in short spells and with the licence to bowl as fast as possible, without consideration of runs. A **stock bowler** performs the opposite function, bowling many overs and conceding as few runs as possible.

Tail-ender: A cricketer with limited batting ability who is very low down his side's **batting order** (the sequence in which players bat). Many, but not all, bowlers are tail-enders. Tail-enders as a group are called the **tail** or the **lower order**. A particularly poor tail-ender is a **rabbit**, or a **bunny**. The worst batsman in the side is sometimes a **ferret** – because he goes in after the rabbits. If the lower order manages to score runs the tail might be said to **wag**.

Ton: One hundred runs.

Topspinner: A slow bowler's delivery with considerable top spin, it dips early and bounces high. Can be bowled by both wrist and finger spinners.

Trundler: A medium-pace bowler who, while reliable, is neither fast nor dangerous. He might be said to bowl **military medium**. If a bowler is worse than a trundler he may be a **dobber** or even a **dibbly dobbly**.

Yorker: A ball that pitches in the block hole, on or near the batsman's feet. In Australia, a Yorker that creeps under the batsman's bat is a **gozunder**.

Zooter: A delivery bowled out of the back of the hand by a leg-spinner. Appears similar to an orthodox leg-spin delivery, but doesn't turn and goes straight on. Named by Shane Warne, its inventor.